Freeman

the agriculture years

Secretary of Agriculture Orville L. Freeman, 1963

Freeman

the agriculture years

1961–1969

Rodney E. Leonard

Hubert H. Humphrey School of Public Affairs
Minneapolis
2015

On the cover
Governor of Minnesota Orville L. Freeman with U.S. Senator John F. Kennedy
before Kennedy's election to the presidency, October 1960

Photo Sources
All illustrations courtesy of Jane Freeman

Copy-editing, design, production
E. B. Green Editorial, St. Paul, Minnesota

Indexing
Patricia Green, Homer, Alaska

Printing and binding
Sexton Printing, Inc., St. Paul, and Muscle Bound Bindery, Minneapolis

© 2015 by Hubert H. Humphrey School of Public Affairs
University of Minnesota
301 19th Avenue South
Minneapolis, MN 55455

Contents

Acknowledgments

Rodney E. Leonard served as Orville L. Freeman's press secretary when Freeman was governor of Minnesota and when he was U.S. secretary of agriculture (1961–1969). Rod's firsthand view as well as his insight, research, and communicative skills led to his role as principal author of this book as well as of his earlier work—*Freeman: The Governor Years, 1955–1960.*

Research and writing are hard work, and Rod worked very hard to give us this volume. In doing so he made much use of facilities and assistance from the USDA's National Agricultural Library in Washington, D.C., the John F. Kennedy Presidential Library and Museum in Boston, the Lyndon Baines Johnson Presidential Library and Museum in Austin, Texas, and the Minnesota Historical Society's Reference Library at the Minnesota History Center in St. Paul.

Special acknowledgment is due Prof. Robert Kudrle of the Hubert H. Humphrey School of Public Affairs at the University of Minnesota in Minneapolis. His editing and assistance in the logistical aspects of bringing this book to life were critical. Without his enormous contribution, you would not be reading this work.

But the soul and inspiration for this book is Jane Freeman, loving and loyal spouse for 60-plus years to Orville Freeman. She was the original force behind this project, and when it seemed to falter, she simply would not let it go. At 94 years young, Jane Freeman today remains an inspiration not only to the extended Freeman and Leonard families but also to hundreds of other dedicated public servants.

—Constance and Michael Freeman

Freeman

the agriculture years

Prologue

Orville L. Freeman, the Minnesotan who served Presidents John F. Kennedy and Lyndon B. Johnson as secretary of agriculture (1961–1969), was a strong, innovative leader. He lived and served in a period of challenges, change, and progress.

He said what he was going to do and did what he said.

There is no argument Freeman changed the political arc of the U.S. Department of Agriculture (USDA), the oldest domestic cabinet agency. The USDA became a different place with a different mission under his direction. Moreover, the organization and structure of the agency have remained largely unchanged since Freeman left office.

The United States has had a secretary of agriculture since Abraham Lincoln established the department in 1861 early in his first term as president. Lincoln also established the land-grant college system, an instrument of education introducing science and technology as the guiding spirit of America, in support of the new department.

Today some 36 or more federal agencies and offices report to the secretary of agriculture. These agencies represent the institutional responsibilities assigned by Congress over the past 150 years to the Department of Agriculture, from the time farming included more than two-thirds of American families. Today farming is an occupation claimed by only 2 million people, of whom fewer than 200,000 grow about 90 percent of the food and fiber produced in the United States.

The social, cultural, and economic changes illuminated by these numbers are massive, especially those occurring at the end of World War II. The United States had preserved democracy in the world but could not end hunger at home. It had produced the materials arming the winners of the war and swiftly refocused the manufacturing economy, but it could not manage the cornucopia of postwar agriculture, the overwhelming surpluses, that ultimately threatened to destabilize the farm economy.

Both issues—hunger and surplus—were uniquely the responsibility of agriculture policy and the secretary of agriculture, though the secretary lacked the authority to manage either issue. Neither Congress nor the president could agree on solutions or authorize action to manage either challenge. In effect, after 100 years as a cabinet agency, the department could not reach within itself for past experience to guide policymakers or the public; neither could the nongovernmental institutions created to manage the agricultural economy go outside the box to offer guidance.

Without stating the obvious, the nation was asking for a secretary to take agriculture into a new era in which access to food was the primary mission. Defining the role of diet, health, and nutrition and the capacity to produce food and fiber without constantly threatening the economic stability of rural America was the primary task. Agriculture was a task of resource management, and food was a policy issue of broad public interest.

The nation required a new farm policy and a new food policy, and therefore a secretary of agriculture who was both innovator and manager.

In 1960, John F. Kennedy was elected president, the first of his generation chosen to lead the nation. In filling the cabinet position for agriculture secretary, Kennedy creatively selected Orville L. Freeman, governor of Minnesota. Freeman had made his reputation in postwar America as a political leader who governed outside the box. He led by creating political space for innovation in public policy while inviting the public to bring new ideas and concepts to, and to participate in, governance. Freeman matured as a leader by developing the organizational capacity and political skills to transform innovation into programs, thus enabling the public good to flourish.

This book examines how Freeman brought innovative leadership to the creation of national food policy and programs to end chronic hunger and malnutrition. Freeman led a furious eight-year political battle in Congress and across the nation to adopt a farm policy for managing abundance. This enabled the people and farmers of the United States to gain control over a highly prolific system of producing food and fiber without the constant threat of surplus. He did what no secretary of agriculture had done before.

The Department of Agriculture Freeman left in 1969 was very different from the agency he found when he arrived in Washington, D.C., in 1961.

Ironically, the department today is essentially unchanged in structure and responsibility from the organization in place when Freeman left in January 1969. But the political and policy horizons of the secretary of agriculture in 2015 are dramatically altered. That situation is due in part to changes in American governance that began after 1970 with the evolution of the presidency and the change in relationship between the president and the cabinet officers. The power and authority of the president has grown, dramatically increasing the power of the executive branch in the White House and the offices and agencies of the Office of the President.

The president's staff today values cabinet officers, particularly cabinet officers of domestic agencies, as managers of huge bureaucracies. Policy innovation is the task of political advisers and political staff members who hold cabinet officers accountable for management failure and errors. The relationship between the president and the cabinet officers has changed in this operational environment. The president shares one limitation with everyone else: each has no more than 24 hours in a day. The president's time is so extraordinarily valuable today that cabinet-officer time with the president is extremely limited.

Freeman skillfully managed his relationship with the White House and his time with two presidents, ensuring that the president desire any controversy generated by Freeman and that it serve a useful political purpose. Freeman's understanding of the structure of Congress and his ability to earn the trust of key leaders were critical to the changes occurring between 1961 and 1969. His innovations, both programmatic and managerial, remain core elements in the nation's agricultural, food, and rural development policies.

Gov. Orville L. Freeman with U.S. Sen. John F. Kennedy in October 1960. Kennedy wrote on the photo: "To Orville Freeman—who ploughs a straight furrow and a long one—with esteem and very best wishes, John F. Kennedy."

1

Awakening

Few people were awake early enough on any morning to roust Orville L. Freeman from bed, but when the phone rang early in Minneapolis on a cold day in December 1960, the caller was John F. Kennedy, who had miles to go before he slept.

"Orv, I want you to be secretary of agriculture," Kennedy said from Washington, D.C. "How soon can you get down here so we can announce it?"

Still groggy but awakening fast, Freeman answered, "I can be down there late this afternoon, Mr. President." He would be the first governor to occupy the secretary's office in the century-old U.S. Department of Agriculture (USDA). Earlier it was the lair of farm journalists, college presidents, farm organization leaders, farm politicians, agricultural scientists, and assorted other notables.[1]

Freeman had been expecting an invitation from the president-elect to join the New Frontier in Washington, but he had said explicitly that he preferred any other office to that of leading the USDA. It would be a thankless job. Farm policy was broken, and a national food policy did not exist. Mountains of surplus grain were piling up unsold on city streets in the Midwest while millions of Americans were hungry. Income in rural areas was low enough in some regions to qualify rural America as a developing country.

Nonetheless, Freeman did not plead with Kennedy for another job. As a former U.S. Marine, wounded by a sniper's bullet on patrol on Bougainville Island in New Guinea during World War II, he accepted the wish of his commander in chief. His favorite phrase was "carry on," and his posture in addressing a challenge was to confront it.

Governor Freeman called the commander of the Minnesota National Guard to request an Air National Guard jet to fly him to Washington. He thought the request of the president-elect for his presence in Washington justified the use of public property for the four-hour flight.

So began Freeman's eight-year odyssey, cementing his place in Minnesota history as a political leader who viewed politics as a noble profession and in U.S. history as a political manager giving new life and a new future to one of the country's oldest government agencies. Freeman put in place farm policy ending mountainous surpluses, created a national food policy ending chronic malnutrition, modernized USDA administrative procedures by computerizing payrolls and management systems, saved India from a famine, brought farmer interests to the negotiating table on global trade policy, changed forestry policy to protect millions of acres of forest wilderness from exploitation, and began building an economic infrastructure in rural areas beyond agriculture.

The USDA observed its sesquicentennial anniversary in 2012, some 150 years after President Abraham Lincoln celebrated the department by signing the legislation granting homesteads to individuals and families and creating land-grant colleges and universities to provide research support and education to the agricultural economy that followed. This system was transformed in the 1930s by the New Deal legislation signed by President Franklin D. Roosevelt and again in the 1960s. The most recent transformation—more than 50 years ago—was profound. The programs adopted then remain the essential policy framework for food, farming, and rural economic development today.

Policy change is a continuing process—a boisterous, noisy collision of economic and social interests and priorities. No system of democratic governance exists for very long without it. The story of Orville Freeman at the USDA reveals the transformation of five decades past that brings us to where we are today and shows us how to "Carry On."

Gov. Orville L. Freeman waves to delegates at the 1960 Democratic Convention after nominating Sen. John F. Kennedy for president.

2

Taking Over

The story of Orville L. Freeman at the USDA must be understood in the context of the 1960 Democratic National Convention in Los Angeles, which nominated John F. Kennedy. However many potential running mates were in contention as the convention started, Kennedy had two men primarily in mind for the vice presidency when the nominations began. He telegraphed one of his choices in the person he asked to put his name in nomination—Orville L. Freeman, the governor of Minnesota. His other choice was Lyndon B. Johnson (D-TX), the Senate majority leader and ultimately the one chosen.

As the convention began, Kennedy thought he would win the nomination. His selection of a running mate would have little bearing on the outcome of the vote count. He did not need the support of the delegates committed to Johnson or Freeman's liberal followers. He had already wrested control of the convention from the city bosses and labor leaders by defeating their preferred candidates in preconvention maneuvering, including the presidential primaries. The Minnesota delegation had fragmented into warring camps, as it was prone to do.[1] It would support Kennedy only after the nomination was won. And Johnson's supporters were conservative Democrats who could mount only token opposition.

The task for Kennedy was to begin shaping the government he would bring to Washington in January 1961. The first step was to select a vice president, the person who would inherit the power of the presidency should the worst occur. Kennedy had observed Johnson in the majority leader's masterly control of the U.S. Senate, and he understood that Johnson would operate in the Senate as an independent power base in a Kennedy administration.

Kennedy had carefully vetted Orville Freeman, repeatedly sending Harvard economist and trusted policy adviser John Kenneth Galbraith to assess the Minnesotan's political philosophy, management competence, and leadership qualities. Kennedy also sent his most trusted political and personal adviser, Ted Sorensen, to evaluate Freeman's personal qualities, his sense of mission as a leader of the new Democratic majority emerging in postwar America, and his compatibility with others who would surface in a Kennedy administration.

No two men appeared to be less alike that Kennedy and Freeman. But they were alike in their pride in public service, in their political sensibilities, in their drive to succeed, and in their personal courage. Each was secure in the knowledge forged in World War II combat that he was living out a second chance at life.

Kennedy invited Johnson to join him on the 1960 Democratic ticket, saying Freeman was his choice should the Texan decline.[2] This left Johnson to conclude that his selection was a political decision based on the belief that he could deliver Democratic majorities in the southern states. Johnson accepted.

Robert F. (Bobby) Kennedy, the nominee's brother and campaign manager, bitterly opposed Johnson's position on the Democratic ticket. Jack Kennedy soothed his brother's anger by saying that he too was surprised by Johnson's acceptance of the invitation, but there was no going back. Before Jack Kennedy announced his decision to the convention, he told Freeman that he based his choice on a desire to keep Johnson close as vice president in the Old Executive Office Building rather than deal with him as Senate majority leader.

The history of the 1960 Democratic National Convention is essential to an assessment of Orville Freeman because when he was sworn in as the secretary of agriculture, President Kennedy and Vice President Johnson knew his name. The members of Congress whom Freeman must persuade to support USDA programs knew that when Freeman spoke to them, he was speaking for the president. USDA employees, listening to Freeman speak about the department's goals and objectives, knew he was speaking for the president, that he had access to the White House and could use it to further department purposes and goals.

Years later, when asked to identify the most outstanding secretary of agriculture he had known, Rep. Jamie L. Whitten (D-MS), chair of the House Appropriations Committee from 1979 to 1993, paused before responding. Whitten had been elected to Congress in 1938, and he chaired the House Agriculture Subcommittee on Appropriations for nearly 20 years before Freeman became secretary. Few House members were as powerful as he, especially in regard to agriculture, and Whitten knew more about agriculture programs than anyone— agriculture secretaries included.

"There were Jardine and Wallace," Whitten said, "and there was this young fellow from Minnesota—Freeman. The president knew his name."[3]

Orville Freeman brought unique skills and managerial experience to his work as secretary. His experience as governor of Minnesota was invaluable. The office had provided him the training ground of an executive and shown him the importance of building political linkages with the legislature (and, later, with Congress).

The USDA was among the oldest of cabinet departments, especially among those with a specific national constituency. Created in 1862 by Lincoln, the first Republican elected president, it fulfilled his campaign promise to create a system of land grant colleges. Other legislative actions included the Homestead Act, a statute opening westward settlement by awarding settlers 160 acres of public land in exchange for farming on and improving it. The department is the only agency of cabinet rank located on the Washington Mall. In choosing Freeman as secretary of agriculture, President Kennedy found an individual who combined six indispensable qualities:

1. Room to maneuver: Kennedy's trust of Freeman, based on a personal relationship understood by the immediate staff members of both men, created a working environment that gave Freeman a free hand to propose policy in program management and congressional relations.
2. A national sense of leadership: Freeman's confidence that he could run a sprawling federal agency was based on his success in running a state government.
3. A political instinct for establishing priorities and planning strategies for USDA programs: From the start, Freeman understood the importance of developing a rapport with the congressional committees, members, chairs, and ranking opposition members.
4. A passionate belief that government is an instrument of change with the potential for enhancing the public good. After WWII, American citizens recognized that if the federal government could organize and manage resources to eliminate threats to survival, it could also build a society able to realize the goals laid down in the Declaration of Independence. The

Democratic–Farmer–Labor Party's [DFL's] emergence as the dominant political power in Minnesota showed that building public support was the first step in creating an environment in which new ideas could grow and public services could thrive.

5. A profound distaste for ideological solutions—specifically, the realization that communism was not a component of, but rather a threat to, democracy.

6. A personality willing to take chances but harnessed by a disciplined intellect that assembled all available information into a linear analysis to produce detailed plans of action.

The challenges Freeman faced as secretary tested those qualities:

- Freeman's predecessor, Ezra Taft Benson, Eisenhower's secretary of agriculture, left the USDA traumatized, aimless, and operating as a collection of uncoordinated bureaucratic fiefdoms—the Rural Electrification Administration (REA), U.S. Forest Service (USFS), Agriculture Research (land grant schools), Commodity Distribution, Agriculture Cooperative Service, Agricultural Library, and Economic Research Service, to name but a few—employing 115,000 people.

- Farm policy was in disarray. Benson had tried to eliminate farm-income programs, apparently assuming that farmers would stop producing crop surplus if farm programs did not exist. Corn, feed grains, and wheat were being harvested in record crops, far exceeding storage space and leaving piles of grain on town streets through the Midwest. Freeman's job was to find a better way.

- Congressional committees were all led by Southern Democrats, a highly conservative group of elderly, likeminded individuals, most having gained political power by supporting segregation. They were suspicious of northern liberals and opposed to government programs with a social dimension. Hubert H. Humphrey (D-MN) had come to grief upon his entry to the U.S. Senate by challenging this powerful clique. Its members knew Freeman only as the politically conjoined Minnesota twin.

- Urban members of Congress—that is, big-city Democrats— shunned the agriculture committees, preferring to serve on those more likely to build a legislative record of interest to urban constituencies.

As Freeman joined the Kennedy cabinet in 1961, his political and policy priorities were sevenfold:

1. Quickly assume command of the USDA
2. Even more quickly establish a working relationship with Congress
3. Eliminate farm surpluses without great cost
4. Reduce or eliminate domestic and world hunger
5. Expand the scope of resources and their availability to the rural economy to increase nonfarm jobs and rural community development
6. Enhance food-safety and food-quality regulatory programs
7. Increase conservation of soil, water, and forestry resources.

One might call that a mighty big agenda!

Rep. Robert Michel (R-IL) presented Secretary of Agriculture Freeman with a framed copy of this cartoon from the Peoria Journal Star, *with this inscription: "Well you did it, Mr. Secretary, with a vote of 211 to 203, April 8, 1964, from your friendly adversary Robert H. Michel, 18th Dist., Ill."*

3

Inventing American Food Policy

The 1960s were a cauldron of often mindless violence. More than 58,000 Americans, mostly young men drafted into military service, died in Vietnam for a cause ultimately abandoned. In addition, churches in which black families worshiped in the South were burned, and young black girls who died there became symbols of racism and oppression.

Black students seeking to enroll in southern universities and colleges were shot and killed. In the name of segregation, southern racists murdered both white and black Americans working to register voters. John F. Kennedy was the only American president assassinated in the 20th century. His brother, Robert F. Kennedy, was shot and killed while campaigning to become president. Martin Luther King, a preeminent American minister, was martyred and became a symbol of America's coming of age in civil rights.

Hunger was another form of violence in the United States as the 1960s began. It was a daily experience shared by more than 40 million people in America. They were mostly white, but many were black or Hispanic. All were impoverished. Many were children, a greater percentage of who lived in poverty and felt hunger more than adults. Hunger visited the elderly who were poor in greater number proportionally than in the population as a whole.

The face of hunger changed constantly. Even the estimate of 40 million hungry Americans was misleading—surely there were more. Poverty was a constant in the calculus of hunger, but a person or family poor one year might escape poverty the next. Someone else, another family, would replace them, the roundelay endlessly replayed.

This matrix of silent hunger rose to a scale that might be overcome only through a national food policy, which then did not exist. While the end of poverty might also end hunger, the concept of poverty aroused passionate argument that provided no solution. Sharing the cornucopia of food abundance, however, was a different matter. If American farmers could produce more food than the nation could consume or sell abroad, then the United States could share the food with the hungry people who could not afford it.

This was the situation within which Secretary Freeman began to articulate a national food policy—redefining hunger and committing the agriculture budget to the funding and operation of a set of food programs—while developing the institutional framework for the policy along with the skills, procedures, and techniques for managing programs that had not existed before. Thus the 1960s will be remembered for violent change but also as the time when the right to food became a social obligation, giving form to a new national goal centered in the Department of Agriculture—ending chronic hunger in every community, in every family, and among all people. Before the decade ended, the tools were in place, and the programs were in operation. (For a short history of previous government food initiatives, see Appendix A.)

Defining hunger

The U.S. Supreme Court, if asked, probably would define hunger as a situation people know when they see or feel it, a recognizable condition in society. Nutritionists prefer to say that hunger is a chronic condition due to a lack of food that may lead to malnutrition. Neither definition is much help to planners and managers in government agencies operating programs to end hunger, which was the case in 1961 when Orville Freeman became the secretary of agriculture.

Hunger happens to people. A mandate for ending hunger means policies and programs that help people who are hungry and that can reach out to them wherever they may be. From that perspective, defining hunger is relatively simple. Hunger is a condition affecting the health of people in definable social or cultural groups in society, such as families and other households, children in school or organized community activities, mothers and their infants and young children, and older persons, especially those who are retired.

This definition of hunger emerged from experience and practice, and it suggested a framework for organizing and financing the delivery of services. Food programs clearly combine elements of education, health, and welfare, but they are none of those alone. In 1961 the federal programs and legislative committees responsible for health, education, and welfare services might have claimed jurisdiction for food programs, but none did—for several reasons.

None had the budget resources to operate and service food programs, and each had bureaucratic and cultural biases that would have challenged food program funding as diverting resources from established priorities. Neither did any federal agency have the managerial skills or administrative experience to operate food programs. Further, the only funding stream in the federal budget that had not been tapped to support social goals for the general public—by then largely urban—was agriculture.

These material factors had to be taken into account in planning a national food policy, but strangely, no one in the Kennedy administration or Congress raised them for discussion. Orville Freeman, as he had done all his political life, invented as he went along, creating new processes, policies, and procedures of governance necessary to ensuring a cohesive, functioning government and building public confidence during a time when the rules were being rewritten.

In the space of a decade, Freeman put national food policy in place, funded through the agriculture budget. Astonishingly, its operation was not achieved through a new USDA bureaucracy. Instead, the food stamp program was run through the existing state system for family services, school meals programs operated through state educational systems, and the Women, Infant, and Children program (WIC) became an integral part of state and local health services for women and children. In effect, food policy emerged as a system for reaching out to people in whatever social environment defined their lives.[1]

Where's the Money?

Before 1961 the only postwar movement in Congress toward a national food policy occurred when Sen. Allen Ellender (D-LA) authorized legislation in 1946 to provide a subsidy of 4.5 cents for every lunch served in American schools. Ellender said he was concerned about the high rate of rejection of young men drafted for military service in World War II. They were underweight, malnourished, or limited physically—conditions related to poor diets caused by chronic hunger in draftees who grew up in the Great Depression.

The agriculture appropriations committees, seemingly appalled at spending agriculture funds for health purposes, did not raise lunch subsidies until Freeman asked them to do so 15 years later. Nevertheless, Ellender's legislation was a precedent for using USDA appropriations explicitly for health policies for the general public, and that was important.

Members of the House and Senate agriculture committees jealously guarded the agriculture budget, seeking to limit appropriations to clearly defined programs servicing farmers and the agricultural community. The House Agriculture Committee, for example, said in 1952 that it did not want authority for school meals. It transferred the program to the Committee on Education and Labor during the same period when Congress approved Senator Ellender's legislation on school lunch subsidies.

The Senate, as it often does, chose not to follow the House, leaving the Senate Agriculture Committee with jurisdiction for a school food service. Ironically, in ceding its jurisdiction for a USDA program, the House Agriculture Committee also established another precedent—a legislative basis for transferring food programs and policy to the jurisdiction of other committees of Congress.

There is good reason for a conservative stance on agriculture appropriations. Under current rules of Congress, the agriculture budget is technically one of the wealthiest budget streams among the arcade of spigots for allotting federal monies. When Congress was raising high tariff walls in 1930 under the Smoot-Hawley Act, the question arose as to the future division of customs receipts for U.S. imports. With high tariffs in a depressed economy, however, the income from customs receipts was small, not worth a major political fight over allocation.

Agricultural interests insisted that a portion of customs income be earmarked specifically for agriculture programs, proposing a division according to their belief that one in three Americans then lived on farms. Congressional negotiators accepted the proposal and the division, though demographers—not then consulted—would have placed the farm population at close to only 20 percent, or one in five.

The revenue division apparently was not a major issue at a time of limited global trade, but the situation today is vastly different. Under the division agreement with the agriculture bloc, Congress authorizes one-third of customs receipts from the preceding fiscal year as new obligation authority (NOA) for the agriculture appropriations committees as authorized under Section 32 of the amended Agricultural Adjustment Act of August 24, 1935.

Technically, NOA is the category of general funds (taxes, levies, fines, or other receipts) in the U.S. Treasury available for newly authorized spending, but only the appropriations committees can obligate it. This rule separates the authorizing committees (intent to spend) from the appropriations committees (how much to spend). Section 32 fences off a portion of those funds for the agriculture bloc.

Given the current level of global trade, Section 32 annually pours $600 million to $700 million into funds ostensibly reserved for the agriculture bloc. Each year the Senate Appropriations Committee formally unblocks the portion of Section 32 funds not spent for USDA programs and related services to general budget use, but it retains the NOA language.

Designating Section 32 monies as NOA was important in the 1930s to those wanting to set aside part of the federal budget for farming and ranching, but the action created unanticipated maneuvering dimensions in the strategies to develop U.S. food policy. NOA is arcane language that essentially allows the House and Senate to bypass the appropriations process. If the agriculture bloc wanted to fund programs, Congress could authorize any program with language stating that the program would be funded from Section 32 funds.

In 1961, when Freeman first broached the Kennedy concept of food stamps to Congress, the response in the agriculture committees was frigid, ranging from "It didn't work in the 1930s and won't work now," to "Now isn't the time," to, most commonly, "NO!"

Aware that he couldn't push water uphill, Freeman proposed a demonstration project of programs at 10 sites across the United States, funded by Section 32 monies. Opposition to a demonstration project was minimal. Freeman could argue he wanted an opportunity to show the program would work, while the opposition believed the program would fail as its depression version did, and the legion of fence sitters could avoid a fight over the issue.

Freeman pointed out that Section 32 funds were available and more than adequate to cover the cost, a gentle reminder that the appropriations committees could not delay approval of the project by refusing to authorize funds. For Freeman, the Section 32 route also ensured that work on the project could begin immediately.

The Food Stamp Program

An airplane loaded with symbolism and reporters from nearly every major news organization in the nation's capital rose into the sky over Washington, D.C., early one spring morning in 1962. One passenger was Secretary of Agriculture Orville L. Freeman. Another was Howard Davis, a 25-year USDA employee who had worked in the abbreviated version of a depression-era food stamp program that ended quietly in 1940. He was now managing its reincarnation.

The airliner, one of the last four-engine, prop-driven planes built by Douglas Aircraft Company, had taken off from a military airfield soon to become a housing development and was headed for an airport near Welch, West Virginia. That the journey was leaving the past behind may have been lost on most passengers, but everyone was aware the plane was flying into Kennedy's New Frontier to dedicate the nation's first food stamp program and observe the start of a national food policy.

The passengers, still queasy from an exceedingly rough landing, loaded themselves into a caravan of buses that wound through the steep hills and narrow valleys of West Virginia to the town of Welch. The hills were dotted with rundown dwellings, mostly unpainted, and behind the depressed towns in the valleys lay the invisible pale of poverty.

The passengers saw the reality that shocked Kennedy in his 1960 campaign and led him as president to say in his first executive order that America had an obligation to make food more available. The order used his executive powers to expand the package of surplus food commodities given by the USDA to the states to distribute to the poor. The news that the USDA was developing a food stamp program beginning with a 10-project demonstration—one of them in Welch—followed.

The 1938 food stamp program was introduced just after misguided economic policies of the Roosevelt administration reversed a sputtering recovery, sending the U.S. economy into the second phase of the Great Depression. The program disappeared in 1940 as massive federal spending for the industrial buildup for World War II kick-started a flood of new jobs. The timely and welcome development also buried the need for an investigation of fraud and other abuses that appeared as the program expanded.

As the term *food stamp* suggests, the original program provided eligible participants with workbooks of pages with outlined space for placing stamps. Participants received set amounts of blue and red stamps each month. Red stamps could be used to purchase surplus food, mostly nonperishable commodities. Blue stamps could be used for non-surplus foods, mostly perishable products, including beef and pork. Food retailers were reimbursed according to the value of the books of stamps they submitted to the federal government.

The system was an administrative monster, not only for the participants who had to lick and fix each stamp in the stamp book but also for merchants and centers for redemption. The opportunities for fraud were legion, with participants happy to redeem stamps for cash but also for merchants to discount the cash value of stamps. No system to monitor the process was active, and no experience served as a basis for training program workers or guiding management.

The food stamp program has evolved over three stages of management reform. At the beginning in 1961, Secretary Freeman made the deliberate decision to emphasize the prevention of fraud, that is, to prevent the illegal sale and purchase of stamps for cash. His decision enabled food stamps to avoid the fate of the early version introduced in 1938.

An intensive educational program was developed in 1961 in cooperation with the Treasury Department to explain the program's internal operating procedures to bankers, food stores, and supermarkets. The program was designed to ensure that the U.S. banking system could process food stamp certificates as easily as regular currency. Certificates worth $1, $5, and $10, and similar in size to U.S. currency, were issued to participants who use them to purchase all food except those, such as alcohol, prohibited by Congress. A significant portion of the time explaining the new program was devoted to spelling out the criminal penalties for fraud, such as discounting the certificates for cash, and describing the intensive enforcement planned by the USDA and the U.S. Treasury.[2]

In retrospect, the initial food stamp program developed by the USDA seems designed to discourage participation. The program was intended to ensure that an eligible person or family could buy a month's worth of food for no more than 30 percent of the current poverty income level. According to many experts, most individuals and families living in poverty were spending up to 60 percent or more of their income for food. The idea was to raise the food budget for individuals and families living in poverty.[3]

The intention was worthy, but the concept was unsettling to many, especially those citizens wanting to verify the practice. The result was the requirement that a monthly allotment of food stamps worth 30 percent of the current poverty level for individuals and families, by family or household size, could be purchased for cash at a price equal to 30 percent of the verified income for the individual or family. In effect, the program captured at the beginning of each month a substantial portion of the monthly cash available to individuals and the family. This restricted their flexibility to cope with emergencies or unanticipated priorities.

Applicants for food stamps virtually had to claim and prove that they were chronically indigent. Application forms were long, confusing, and complicated, which created an informal demand for a new job skill in filling out and negotiating program applications. When Congress authorized the three-year-old food stamp demonstration program in 1964 as a federal entitlement, limits on personal possessions were attached. For example, applicants could possess automobiles, but only those valued under $2,000. These were the cars of individuals who often had no access to public transportation to the places where jobs could be found.

In authorizing food stamps in 1964 as a service available to all citizens, Congress made access geographically limited to state and local governments willing to accept and operate the program. Ironically, the House and Senate agriculture committees with food stamp program jurisdiction also were authorizing and funding federal programs in every state to subsidize income for farmers, to protect the water and soil resources needed to farm, and to fund universities and colleges to educate all citizens, including farmers. Every state and local government would demand that the federal government provide these programs without restricting access.

Conditional access meant Secretary Freeman and program managers had to devote resources to prying open the rights of citizens to food stamps. From a practical perspective, concerted attention was required in the southern states, especially Mississippi, Alabama, and South Carolina. But county governments scattered locally through rural America—in Pennsylvania, Wisconsin, Montana, and elsewhere—were equally obdurate about controlling access to food.

If Congress believed conditional access was an effective strategy to slow public acceptance of food stamps, the tactic actually had the opposite effect. Where food program advocacy groups had criticized the USDA and the White House for moving too slowly after 1961, the same organizations targeted state, city, and county officials and agencies after 1964 with demands and political pressure to adopt the food stamp program.

The energy of advocates caught state and local governments in a vise. The executive branch pushed from the top down as citizen organizations, the press, and the public pushing locally from the bottom up. Within three years, every state government had created food stamp program units within its state welfare agencies. And food stamps were available in every major urban area and city and in more than half of all U.S. counties.

The impact of the shift in focus may have seemed spotty when viewed as food stamp availability on a map of U.S. counties. But the consequences were impressive to budget analysts. The food stamp program passed the initial billion-dollar milestone in fiscal 1968—the first food program to reach the billion-dollar marker in USDA history.[4]

While the milestone was only casually observed, by implication the USDA and agriculture committees of Congress had crossed a new policy threshold. From this point forward, food programs and food policy dominated food and farm policy. As if to inadvertently confirm that fact, food programs became the dominant legal and litigation effort of the USDA's office of general counsel after 1967.

The mushrooming growth of food stamp participation triggered a second stage in the evolution of the program, which began early in the 1970s and occurred primarily in Congress. As local managers, advocates, and government officials became familiar with the harsh and often administratively senseless conditions and restrictions imposed as legislative mandates by the USDA and Congress, members of Congress began asking questions raised by constituents to justify conditions.

When staff members and leaders of the Senate and House agriculture committees were asked why food stamps were available only in states that chose to offer access but no similar condition was applied to farm subsidies, only lame excuses could be given. When asked to justify the practice of requiring eligible participants to purchase their monthly allotment of food stamps, the answer essentially was that it seemed the right way to run the program. Members of the agricultural committees who insisted on attaching onerous restrictions such as personal property limits in exchange for voting to allow food stamp legislation to be considered by the House or Senate did not overtly oppose the program. But they could wink to friends that the restrictions served the same purpose.

Senators Robert J. Dole (R-KS) and George S. McGovern (D-SD) were both members of the Senate Agriculture Committee; they also cochaired the Senate Hunger Committee. Working together, they led the change, stripping away many of the onerous and indefensible provisions of the food stamp program. In 1973, for example, Dole introduced legislation mandating that food stamps be available to all eligible individuals and families regardless of their residence, and both senators worked to eliminate the monthly purchase requirement that reduced the ability of families to manage their cash resources.

When Hubert Humphrey returned to the Senate and the Senate Agriculture Committee in 1972 after serving as vice president, another strong voice arrived for food stamps and food programs, particularly for guiding the legislative transition of the demonstration phase of the WIC program to status as permanently authorized food policy.

The second phase of the food stamp program illustrates the penchant of legislators and managers to create programs that serve their convenience rather than the people the program is intended to serve. From the standpoint of program managers, acknowledging that long, complex, and invasive application forms can be simplified and shortened allows managers to be accommodating while maintaining the dominant role in a power relationship. The less preferred option for managers is to be in a defensive position with critics who complain that managers are complacent in failing to collect the information needed to protect taxpayers.

The initial effort to capture all of the cash that participants were required to pay to "buy" the food stamp bonus was senseless and invasive. Once data on individual or household income was obtained, the amount of bonus food stamps could be calculated and made available without further action. Forcing participants to "buy" the benefits provided by statute underscored another penchant of lawmakers and managers to impose unwritten behavioral controls—in this case, specifying monthly spending for food regardless of unpredictable monthly demands on household cash.

Early on, the perceptions among food stamp participants sharply contrasted with those of lawmakers and public officials who assumed food stamps were another form of welfare. For food stamp participants, the program was a coping mechanism for individuals and households to navigate between near poverty and poverty, a status determined by unpredictable income and uncertain jobs. Restrictions on the value of personal property was a conventional view held by public officials and many citizens who believed poverty was a chronic condition of a class of individuals and families. Such restrictions created great difficulties for the individuals and households valuing food stamps as a coping mechanism.

This tug of policy wars between public officials and a growing universe of citizens who valued coping mechanisms occurred in the midst of the 1980s economy, in which middle-class income ceased growing. At the same time the share of national wealth held by the middle and lower-middle classes also declined. Food stamp participation, as a consequence, continued to grow. And program costs rose, which led conservatives to develop tactics to cut program spending.

Unable to cut funding for food programs, Republicans proposed to convert food program budgets—and other national services—to blocks of federal funds to be given to state governments. Priorities for the use of the block grants were determined by state governors and legislatures, a strategy used to cap federal spending and shrink the federal government. Block grants also enshrined the concept of discrimination as a power of state government to deny access to services depending on geographical residence, without appeal.

Democrats rejected the Republican goals, but Democrats and Republicans agreed on reducing program costs through management reforms and operational efficiencies, which led to the third major change in the food stamp program. Beginning in the 1980s and continuing into the 1990s, an electronic revolution transformed food stamps much the same way that Secretary Freeman computerized the payroll and accounting systems of the department 20 years earlier.

Instead of certificates in denominations of $1, $5 and $10, nearly all participants received plastic money, a debit card linked to individual computer accounts into which the department deposited the monthly bonuses of additional funds to supplement the food budgets of individuals and households participating in food stamp programs. Once a month, food stamp accounts were recharged automatically, and most grocery retailers were equipped to accept the USDA plastic as routinely as a regular plastic money card. Retail accounting systems were programmed to exclude food products that Congress banned from food stamp purchase. Participants could pay cash for those items.

The third generation of change—electronic accounts—revolutionized the food stamp program in many ways at several management and system levels. Eliminating the issuing and processing of billions of paper certificates has saved the USDA and U.S. Treasury tens of millions of dollars in administrative and operational costs as well as in reimbursement to state governments for administrative expenses.

Management of the program became more complex even as the system became more manageable. As the number of individuals and households increased into the tens of millions, the sheer numbers threatened to bog down the capacity of the program to operate and increased its operational and administrative costs. Electronic systems eased record keeping while improving productivity in administrative operations. Using plastic money also minimized the opportunity for fraud and other abuse. Discounting the cash value of debit cards has proved more difficult than under-the-counter sales of certificates, though individual ingenuity cannot be discounted.

The third generation of change in the food stamp program was critical. Without the capacity of the program to expand, its service to nearly 46 million people would not have been possible. Perhaps even more critical than the expansion of managerial capacity was confirmation of the perception that food stamps are a coping mechanism for individuals and families. Debit cards are one form of plastic money, and plastic money is widely used in supermarkets and retail food stores without stigma or distinction as to the source of credit. Everyone is treated alike.

School Meals: The Lunch Programs

Child nutrition has a storied past in school meals—historically it was mostly the brown-bag experience of children hoping their mothers would pleasantly surprise them with the contents of their noon lunch bags. Lunches served in school first appeared as a formal part of ancillary services in public schools in big-city systems in the late 1890s. Meal service exploded as a public school service during and after World War II, when women joined Rosie the Riveter to work in defense plants, replacing the men who had gone off to war.

World War II was instrumental in the creation of school lunch programs for several reasons. By the time Senator Ellender introduced the first federal funding for school lunch programs in 1964, the wartime growth of school lunch programs had created a clearly needed and popular nutrition system. Ellender's legislation directing the USDA to create a program to give cash to public and private schools for food service was pivotal and established precedence.

The USDA had been sending surplus commodities for several years to state educational agencies to distribute to local schools and school districts, an activity that made senators and members of Congress from rural states and congressional districts happy. They could boast to constituents and fellow legislators about how kindhearted they were.

Sending cash was something entirely different. First, many senators and members of the agriculture committees had different priorities for cash, preferring especially the projects that farmer constituents wanted funded. Second, if the agriculture budget could be diverted to funding nutrition in schools, more funding would follow—not only to schools but also to other socially progressive programs. Ellender had opened a door in the wall of agricultural indifference that a truck could drive through.

In fact, Secretary Freeman drove a convoy of programs to children in American schools through Ellender's opening. In 1960 public schools struggled to come to terms with a demographic constant that prevails today—the number of children growing up in poor families is larger in proportion to the number of children growing up in American families overall than the number of children growing up otherwise (poor families have more children). Nearly one-quarter of children in school today are living in poverty, and they are more likely to be malnourished than their peers.

School lunches today are a major source of nutrition for children in school, but in 1960 poor families could not afford the cost of lunches even with the 4.5 cents of Ellender's subsidy, which inflation had largely eroded. And schools could not afford to make up the difference between the Ellender funds and the cost of lunches charged to students and families.

In 1962 Freeman proposed a USDA budget including a major increase in school lunch funding. A new schedule of reimbursements included categories for all lunches served, for lunches served to children in families with incomes below 175 percent of poverty, and for lunches served to children in families with incomes below poverty. Lunches served to all children were to be reimbursed at the rate of 28 cents each. Reimbursements were set to ensure that meals were served at nominal or no cost to the children of families qualifying for higher reimbursement.

Currently the school lunch program funds lunches served daily to more than 38 million children in public and private schools, with nearly two of every three children receiving lunches at no cost to their families.

School Breakfast

Soon after more resources began flowing to schools for expanding lunch services, information began to accumulate on a major deficiency in child nutrition services, some from surveys by USDA staff and some from reports from school officials. Essentially they all said the same thing: to keep pace with growing living costs, both parents of many families were working.

Families with working parents created a major problem for schools and teachers. Parents were leaving an increasing number of children outside school in the early morning hours. Many of these children had not eaten breakfast. Hungry children were often listless, inattentive in class, and falling asleep at their desks. They were waiting for lunch to get their first meal of the day. Education had to wait until hunger was appeased.

Schools could open their doors earlier than usual, but school administrators had no staff to supervise the early children, and they felt imposed upon to provide childcare services. And, while schools had cafeterias in which they could serve breakfast, no funds were available to pay for it. The obvious question came to Secretary Freeman's desk: What could the USDA do to help?

In 1962, Freeman was able to insert language in USDA legislation authorizing school breakfast programs, but the agriculture appropriations subcommittees waited for a year before accepting a line item in the USDA budget to appropriate school breakfast funds. Today, nearly 10 million children in school participate in the breakfast program daily. Almost 8 of every 10 are served the meal at no or nominal cost to their families.

Women, Infants, and Children Program

The WIC program began in the Department of Agriculture after doctors and staff members at neighborhood health clinics complained that many, if not most, mothers and infants they treated were suffering illnesses related to chronic hunger. They were unable to convince health policy experts with other priorities than nutrition to provide budgets that would allow them to prescribe food, save lives, and lower health care costs. Initially the USDA built and funded WIC commissaries in neighborhood clinics stocked with foods designated by clinic staff and purchased by the USDA. Later it switched to a system enabling clinic staff to provide vouchers to mothers for the purchase of healthy baby food from nearby food stores.

Guardians of conventional budget priorities and gatekeepers of policy authority may criticize the WIC program for bypassing the vetting process through which federal programs are traditionally created and established. With WIC program spending rising above $10 billion a year, some health experts with other priorities likely harbor thoughts about whether those billions could be better spent elsewhere. Nowhere in the development of WIC is there literature reflecting meetings, workshops, or conferences of health experts demonstrating that the program has grown out of an exhaustive examination of significant policy and scientific studies. Neither has there been a careful assessment of the most appropriate allocation of resources in the health field about the impact of diet on infants' and mothers' health before the establishment of the WIC program.

The proposal to establish WIC did not arise from an agreement in the health establishment to request action from Congress but rather from the hurly-burly around a need that began among people in neighborhoods and somehow survived its reach through the world of policy and politics. The proposal for neighborhood food commissaries in health clinics did not begin as a submission from the USDA for consideration by the Department of Health, Education, and Welfare (HEW).[5]

Instead, USDA officials were invited to a national meeting of physicians and staff of neighborhood health clinics sponsored by the Bureau of Women and Children, at which they discussed the prevalence of illness treated at clinics as early symptoms of malnutrition. In assent to a question from a USDA official as to whether a food commissary would be a valuable asset, the USDA proposal shortly followed. The grassroots effort essentially faced no opposition.

President Kennedy signing the feed grains bill into law, May 20, 1963 (l-r): Rep. Robert Poage (D-TX), unidentified, Chair of the House Agriculture Sub- committee on Appropriations Harold D. Cooley (D-NC), Chair of the Senate Agriculture Committee Allen Ellender (D-LA), three unidentified, Edward C. Jaenke of the Department of Agriculture, and Secretary of Agriculture Freeman

4

Supply Management

The job of secretary of agriculture in John F. Kennedy's cabinet in 1961 presented a unique challenge wrapped in a conundrum: How could a nation able to produce more food than was needed to supply a healthy diet for every man, woman, and child in America allow 40 million or more to go hungry? President Kennedy, a political leader who confronted challenges, asked Orville Freeman to find the answer.

Oddly enough, the dilemma arose from abundance, a change that at the end of World War II any nation seemingly would welcome. The problem had confounded the USDA, scientists, experts, professional managers, and politicians since before the Great Depression. Yet no playbook to guide policy on abundance was available in 1961. Congress and the previous administrations had assembled the USDA piecemeal over 100 years into a department some four dozen agencies and smaller units, employing more than 125,000 people, including what was probably one of the greatest concentrations of people with doctorates then gathered in a cabinet department.

The department's successes were manifold and astonishing. Its personnel and their predecessors had fulfilled its mission of a century earlier to turn American farms into a vast cornucopia of crops, livestock, fowl, and forests. They had created a system of public universities and colleges peopled with scholars and researchers and equipped with the tools of science and technology. USDA had transformed farming into the science of agriculture. By observing farmers and farming communities, it had learned how to transfer research from the laboratory into farming practices to raise the output of fields, forests, and ranches.

Science and technology were the sorcerer's apprentices, mythical twins who induced the cornucopia to spew an endless stream of food that no one could stop. Farm output rose steadily, rebuffing unpredictable weather to achieve a predictable rise in crop and livestock production that was mathematically precise. Abundance spawned the new profession of agricultural economists, experts who could explain why the farm economy was different, difficult, and unforgiving. Experts could explain why abundance was a mixed blessing and why, for farmers, the pot at the end of the rainbow more often was full of cinders than gold. Agricultural economists could tame the weather by identifying methods to improve efficiency and productivity for individual farms, but they could not engineer away a unique quality of the human stomach that had a devastating impact on farm income.

Simply put, when an individual has consumed a $5 meal, he or she will spurn the offer of a second meal, even at half the price. Or, as an economist might say, food demand is inelastic. So farm prices vary widely. If food supplies are short, people who are hungry will pay dearly for the first meal. Once they are no longer hungry, they will pay next to nothing for a second one.

Farm prices ride a razor's edge between too little and too much.

Abundance was a policy objective of the U.S. government with the implied promise that prosperity awaited the farmer who produced more. But that was before the risk of abundance was understood. The agricultural economist could explain that farm prosperity usually occurs if farm production is smaller than consumer demand. But history before the 20th century showed the effects of scarcity on society: governments learned that shortages in an open society inevitably led to social unrest, revolution, and violent political change.

Abundance was the product of a political decision in 1862 that ended the threat of famine and starvation while improving political stability and supporting the rule of law. A hundred years later a political solution to the cornucopia was needed, but anything stanching the flow of food was unacceptable, and the balance between production and consumption had to be tilted to the supply side of the scale.

The underlying policy objective was to find that elusive balance between farm prosperity and a full stomach in a market economy, a goal that eluded the best efforts of everyone—farm leaders, agricultural experts, agricultural economists, White House advisers, and any and all members of Congress who tried. It eluded everyone.

Even the "ever normal granary" of the biblical Joseph—one that stored grain harvested in the lush years to provide bread during the lean ones—had proven ineffective. In lean years, production grew faster than the number of stomachs to fill. Across the Midwest, the great breadbasket of the United States, grain elevators were full. In the late 1950s there was no place to store wheat, corn, or soybeans.

Rather than celebrating abundance, the American people were appalled during harvest season by the sight of corn being stored in giant piles covered by tarps on the streets of small towns in Iowa, Illinois, and other midwestern states. The grain was vulnerable to rain damage, and losses from spoilage were huge, reducing farmer incomes further.

Abundance revealed the Gordian knot that was Kennedy's political dilemma. Freeman believed he had an answer, one that had been percolating through the profession of agricultural economics since the end of World War II. The idea was simple in concept but profoundly complex in execution, as Freeman discovered.

In 1960 economists at the USDA reported good news that was bad news. Corn production for the biggest U.S. commodity was exceptional. The 1960 harvest was a "record-breaker," achieved with 30 percent fewer farmers and farm workers and on 10 percent fewer acres than would have been the case a decade earlier. But farmers had gained no increase in earnings in 1960, even though farm exports were 18 percent higher and the federal government had continued propping up farm prices by adding to a surplus mountain valued at more than $9 billion and growing—of wheat, butter, cheese, cotton, and most of all, corn.

Food and fiber production had become a national priority in 1862, but Americans had not expected that a good outcome a century later might be a bad experience. The really bad news was the prediction that farmers would have another really good corn harvest in 1961. Willard Cochrane, USDA's chief economist, warned Secretary Freeman, newly appointed by President Kennedy, that the 1961 crop would likely break all records.[1]

The *New York Times,* anticipating that the bad experience of a good outcome might continue, asked leading senators and representatives in Congress in early January 1961 whether changes were likely in farm policy. The legislators said "little in the way of concrete farm legislation" was expected.[2]

The *Times* interviews convinced the newspaper that there was little hope for change: "It may be safely reported that no solutions are in sight." Further, it suggested: "Political leaders [need] to find a way to gear production to consumption and to avoid the continued build-up of surplus food and fiber stock and the heavy outlay of federal subsidies and other farm payments [that] have caused urban complaints."

Neither did the *Times* have much hope for the new Kennedy administration: "The fact that there will be a Democrat in the White

House and a Democratic majority in Congress does not assure quick agreement on farm policy."

Yet within four months, Secretary Freeman proposed and Congress adopted supply management as the basis for U.S. farm programs, a fundamental shift in the nature and purpose of American agricultural policy. Although the details of applying supply management were debated over the following three years, the fight about taking that direction was nearly over before it started. The advice of the *New York Times* in January to "gear production to consumption and to avoid the continued build-up of surplus food and fiber stock" was translated into law before the end of April.

The compelling mandate was not a sudden awakening. The *Times* only summarized an economic consensus that had been reached a decade earlier. Unless Congress adopted new farm legislation before farmers made decisions in April and May on how much corn to plant in 1961, another surplus-producing harvest would be unavoidable.

President Kennedy sent Congress a proposal in early February for an emergency feed-grain program (corn accounts for most feed-grain output) with a supply management framework. In exchange for a verifiable reduction in the acreage planted to corn, the federal government would put a floor under the price of a bushel of corn. Under previous farm policy, growers had planted unlimited crop acreage with a corn price floor so as to ensure individual farmers an income on par with non-farmers. Essentially, it was a policy based on parity, decidedly not with supply management in mind.

President Kennedy's message to Congress said the emergency program would cut feed-grain output enough to reduce the overall level of feed grain surpluses held in government storage. Further, it would produce combined savings through precluding the cost of additional corn and feed-grains storage and reducing the cost of storing farm surpluses already on hand. Farmers would begin planting the 1961 crop in mid-April, Kennedy said, and they needed to know the details of how they would fare under the terms of the new program. The new program was important to farmers, taxpayers, and all Americans, he said—Congress could authorize the legislation easily by nature's deadline.

The proposal was in fact an enormous gamble. Except for declaring war on Japan on December 8, 1941, a day after Pearl Harbor, Congress had not easily enacted major legislation, never within a two-month time period. Moreover, given the momentum of agricultural productivity and the possibility of weather conductive to plant growth, the voluntary feed-grain program might cost substantially more than estimated. An angry Mother Nature could just as easily add to surpluses and raise storage costs, ending Freeman's tenure as secretary of agriculture in supply-management disgrace.

Kennedy's appeal for quick action galvanized Congress, abruptly ending the casual discourse in Washington policy circles anticipating that the president would move slowly to end the policy deadlock on farm legislation. Congress adopted the emergency feed-grain program and Kennedy signed it into law in fewer than 30 days. Farmers reacted positively, an indication that they welcomed the change in policy and leadership, by pledging to cut corn acreage by more than the Department of Agriculture had hoped.

Freeman and his team of economic planners, led by Cochrane, had begun planning the emergency feed-grain program shortly after Kennedy announced Freeman's designation as the head of the USDA. The emergency program was a voluntary system shorn of the controversial features of the original supply management policy—a program mandating farmer participation.

"I recommended to President Kennedy," Freeman said, "and he agreed, that rather than enact legislation, we would try to set up a procedure to establish farm programs. We would ask for authority similar to [that provided in] the Administrative Procedures Act (APA) [in which] a plan can be proposed to Congress and become law if Congress does not act, [that is] reject the proposal, within a specified time limit."[3]

In proposing the emergency feed-grain program, however, President Kennedy had narrowed the focus on supply management to a gamble on legislation. If the emergency program succeeded, then the debate on supply management would focus on the details of management.

By late summer, the data suggested Kennedy (and Freeman) had won the gamble. As the October corn harvest showed, corn farmers produced less corn for the year than was consumed and exported. This reduced the corn surplus in storage by an estimated 300 million bushels, costing nearly a billion dollars less than budget estimates in absence of supply management.

The struggle, however, was never about the federal budget but rather about whether the United States had the creative imagination and determination to develop and implement public policies grounded in reality. The crisis ended; the creature of abundance was harnessed.

By 1960 abundance was an economic condition that benefitted consumers but had concentrated food production until fewer than two million farms were producing nearly 90 percent of farm output, and the future of those farmers was uncertain. Freeman recognized that two different rural policies were needed. Development of supply management was one. The other was development to create a new rural economy.

The emergency feed-grain program demonstrated that supply management was an economic policy missing in agriculture and that it could be instituted only through the federal government. The unsettled question was what form supply management should take. Crusty Texan Democrat Sam Rayburn, who was speaker of the house, was certain the policy was a legislative prerogative rather than an executive procedure.

As Freeman explained later, proposals to develop programs through executive procedures were not well received in Congress. Rayburn was particularly irritated. "I recall vividly going to his office when he said in no uncertain terms that this would not pass the House even if it got out of committee," Freeman said. "Given the narrow margin at best, that meant that without the speaker, it was dead."[4]

45

Even with that threatening judgment in the background, Freeman continued working to convince members of the House Agriculture Committee to support the proposal that President Kennedy sent to Congress in June for permanent supply-management authority. Mindful of the concern expressed by Rayburn, farmer advisery committees would develop commodity programs with the USDA's advice and counsel, emphasizing that farmers rather than bureaucrats would have the final say before any proposal was sent to Congress for an up-or-down vote. The Kennedy proposal allowed sufficient time for extensive committee hearings in the House and broad public input after a full vetting of program details.

Ken Birkhead, the USDA's legislative director, worked with the White House legislative staff to find a safe majority of senators to vote for the legislation should it reach the Senate floor and, further, a majority of Senate Agriculture Committee members to send the legislation to the full Senate. In the House, the Agriculture Committee would vote to report the supply management proposal to the House floor, and the Rules Committee would authorize a House vote.

An assessment of individual House members, Birkhead concluded, indicated a positive 10-vote margin. He believed four members, under heavy pressure from the Farm Bureau, which was vocally opposed to supply management, were likely to switch from support to opposition should their votes not be needed. At a minimum, the president's proposal would squeak through with a two-vote margin.

Freeman and Birkhead felt the margin was dangerously slim, but they also believed the count was at its peak and unlikely to improve. In fact, support was more likely to erode. Mindful of Rayburn's warning, they also thought Rayburn would not openly undercut legislation representing weeks of hard and difficult organizing by the Democratic majority in the chamber he led as speaker. If Rayburn had made his views known to other House leaders, the fact that legislation reached the House floor at all was evidence that his position had been rejected.

After a long debate that ended late in the evening, the House voted. The legislation was rejected by a two-vote margin. Members of Freeman's staff sat in stunned silence as Birkhead phoned Freeman with the news. Freeman left his office to step into an adjoining room to call President Kennedy, who had also just received account of the vote. Aware the vote was crushing news, Kennedy consoled Freeman, saying he was satisfied the secretary had done all that could possibly be done.[5]

The House vote was a defeat for a procedural option, however, not a rejection of supply management. As this became evident, the gloom hanging over Freeman and his staff lifted, and they started work on an option. Congress had no appetite to return to a parity-based system on corn; neither did opponents of supply management offer other policy options. While Congress dithered, corn growers clearly supported an extension of the voluntary program, a position that led Congress to extend the 1961 program for the 1962 growing season.

Growers of cotton, peanuts, and tobacco, important crops in the Deep South, operated with broadly supported farm programs involving significant federal regulation. The programs, other than cotton, did not generate surpluses requiring federal storage and were not significant budget concerns. Federal programs for these crops were essentially variations of supply management, as was the nation's dairy program, without which most dairy farmers would be unable to survive.

The focus on supply management narrowed to wheat, a crop of which the federal government then held nearly 2 billion bushels in storage. On average, wheat growers produced nearly 1.2 billion bushels of wheat for a U.S. market that consumed half, or no more at most than 700 million bushels. Exports averaged 300 million bushels a year, leaving a substantial volume of wheat for annual purchase by the USDA. Most U.S. wheat today is produced in the Great Plains on high-acreage farms, but in 1961 wheat was also grown widely in small plots in the East and Midwest.

Freeman proposed that Congress authorize a referendum for

wheat farmers to decide whether or not to operate under supply management, in a program that would enable a reduction in both planted acreage and surplus levels, with a floor under market prices. Senators and House members from the Great Plains region—the wheat belt—supported the concept of supply management and the referendum, reflecting the sentiment of the growers who produced most of the wheat in the United States and whose economic survival was linked to federal farm programs.

Congress authorized a referendum in 1963 that subsequently was recognized as a strategic error. Although growers who planted small plots (averaging 15 acres or less) of wheat were not affected by the terms of the referendum, they vastly outnumbered the Great Plains growers who planted thousands of acres and produced the bulk of the U.S. wheat. Mobilized to vote in the referendum, small growers overwhelmed large growers, eliminating the referendum as an option in applying supply management as a farm policy.

The referendum lost, but the returns demonstrated that the American wheat farmer was a giant in two bodies joined at the hip. One farmed in eastern and southern states and typically harvested plots of wheat under 15 acres on diversified farms. The other lived in the West, farming in the wheat belt, harvesting 10,000-acre wheat farms. Both planted wheat but of different varieties, and they were of two minds, depending on geography and its impact on their economic status.

Farmers for whom the wheat harvest determined the annual success or failure of their farming operations strongly supported supply management. Those operating diversified farms, where wheat was not a primary crop, voted strongly against the concept. Senators and House members from the wheat belt, stretching from the high plains of Texas north to the windswept prairies of the Dakotas, knew their constituents wanted supply management as a risk management tool. And knowing their constituents voted in support, those legislators were mostly appalled with the referendum outcome.

President Kennedy and Secretary Freeman were very much aware of the dilemma posed by the two different groups of wheat growers.[6]

Kennedy, looking ahead to his reelection campaign in 1964, wanted to remain flexible. "Any statement opposing another proposal on wheat policy is not sound, for obvious reasons. We couldn't pass any wheat legislation now, however, even if we wanted to propose something," he said.

"I agree," Freeman replied. "We ought to say we had done our best to meet our standards, and the farmer has been unwilling to accept them."

Mischievously, Kennedy asked, "What were those standards?"

"Less cost to the taxpayer, cutting surpluses, and maintaining farm income," Freeman replied. He then moved quickly to outline a possible combined wheat/feed grain program applying the voluntary feature of the current feed grain program.

Kennedy asked for details.

"By maintaining the feed ratio between wheat and feed grains, and by using payments to farmers who agree to limit crop acreage on wheat and feed grain, we would be able to maintain farm income and to hold down production and hope we can cut surpluses," Freeman said.

Kennedy said, "A program next year along the lines you outlined would be highly desirable. We would be able to go to the wheat farmer and agriculture in general and say that our initial program was turned down, but here is another one. If it passed, we would be in good shape. If it didn't, we would be able to say strongly that we had advocated a program [that] would be to their benefit."

The two quickly turned to political strategy and tactics, mindful that during the referendum campaign the president had emphasized that his administration had no backup plan in the event wheat farmers rejected supply management.

This point Freeman made frequently and more directly. He insisted, "We must not deviate from our position of saying no new legislation. In fact, even thinking about such a possibility next year ought to be placed in a dark closet somewhere."

He urged the president not to be influenced too much by some senators, observing that enacting a program would take skillful timing and political maneuvering: "If we hold firm on opposing new legislation this year and indicate there might not be a program next year, while securing support from some who normally would oppose such a program, some Republicans as well as some people linked to the Farm Bureau would be worried."[7]

Opponents as well as supporters agreed on only two matters: First, their lives were dominated by the unresolved question of the role of supply management in U.S. farm policy. Second, all shared a common understanding that the wheat referendum had been the penultimate confrontation. The final confrontation lay ahead, but only the White House would decide when the conflict would begin.

Freeman argued vigorously for a tactical strategy to create uncertainty among Republicans and the Farm Bureau opponents of supply management, forcing the opposition to spend resources and energy to stay united and allow the White House to choose the timing of the next political battle. The tactic would create diversions and division, exploiting Republican fear of losing political support among farmers who wanted a federal program and would become increasingly uneasy the longer its announcement did not come.

The strategy would also create difficulties for Freeman among groups supporting supply management. Their leaders were willing to make the decisions that only Freeman and Kennedy could make. Freeman described a conversation with William (Bill) Thatcher, the imperious president of the Farmers Union Grain Terminal Association (GTA), the cooperative marketing association dominating the upper half of the U.S. wheat-growing region. Thatcher was unquestionably the most powerful individual among wheat growers, and he played a dominant role in the referendum and its approval among midwestern farmers. His command of political power and influence depended on the perception of wheat growers that he could move mountains, including presidents and secretaries of agriculture.

"Thatcher demanded that I not pull the rug out from under him when all we said was [that] we would propose no new program if the referendum did not pass," Freeman told the president. "And now he is beginning to talk about a new program already. So he better keep the rug under me; he need not fear my pulling it out from under him."

Freeman returned to his office in the Department of Agriculture, telling himself, "All in all, the course of action is clear," while putting in motion the planning for legislation that would authorize a permanent, voluntary, supply management program to be introduced in Congress early in 1964.

Freeman summarized the situation succinctly in his Kennedy Library oral history: "By 1963 it was clear that supply management as an executive policy mechanism could not pass Congress. The analysis that mandatory programs were not viable was accurate, but . . . equally accurate was . . . that a federal farm program for farm commodities was essential. In effect, the next step was to create a mechanism that would enable producers of individual commodities to negotiate the details with the federal government—a concept that was agreeable to Congress since the legislative branch would control the process."

That mechanism was supply management—as a legislative process by which Congress would adopt programs to limit production based on USDA data and analysis as to the level of output that would avoid surpluses in commodities. Congressional hearings were no longer a platform on which to debate ideology but rather the arena for negotiation in which producers and producer groups could fix the level of subsidies that would attract the participation of growers. The cost of these negotiations would be incorporated in the legislation approved by Congress and sent to the president, who could sign or veto the legislation.

Orville Freeman had proposed supply management as an executive mechanism by which the president could send Congress a farm program it could adopt or reject within 90 days. A hard-eyed appraisal by farmers revealed that supply management offered them two real choices: Under executive supply management, farmers would not negotiate with the USDA but with the Office of Management and Budget (OMB). Under the legislative version, farmers would negotiate with the people making the final decision on federal budgets. Given the choice, farmers who lived in a democracy would always do better with the people needing their votes.

————

With his initiatives on food stamps and supply management, Freeman recognized that he had turned the department squarely into the wind of change in less than three years and that 1964 was the year to test whether the new direction was permanent. He had one other major awareness: solving the farm problem would expose an economic fault line in rural areas that was currently being ignored.

The introduction of science into agriculture had endowed the United States with the resources to end chronic hunger at home. But the union of scientist (who changed the natural order) and farmer (who found comfort in the natural order) also had the unanticipated effect of turning rural America into the economic equivalent of a third-world nation.

As agriculture became more efficient and productive, one person could farm the land that 10 people farmed earlier, with an output of what 20 farmers had formerly produced. Fewer farmers were needed, as were fewer farm workers, fewer villages and towns, fewer places in which to work, and fewer school districts. As governor of Minnesota, Freeman had confronted the cost of social change with policies for education, public health, cultural opportunities, social services, public services, economic development, and tax programs.

Rural school districts had measurably fewer dollars to spend per student than city and urban districts, resulting in unequal educational programs in the state, a condition discriminating against young people because of where they lived. Rural districts were dependent mainly on property taxes for revenues, while city and urban districts relied on a more diverse tax base. Redistricting to merge schools and school districts reduced overhead costs while raising social tension, and it did nothing to change the underlying unfairness of state policies that put the future of some children at risk. The same pattern of discrimination against rural residents was being repeated in health services, community infrastructure, job opportunities, and other sectors distinguishing the quality of life in a developed nation.

In almost every sector of public policy, political leaders in state and local governments were confronting a pattern of widespread discrimination affecting people who lived in rural areas. This could be traced to federal policy intended as a public good. The tragedy was that the governance system responsible for this anomaly was blind to the nature of the dysfunction, its dimensions, how broadly the dislocation affected society, and to the organization and character of the federal response needed.

If anyone doubted Freeman was an incurable romantic, the notion was dispelled when he began planning his agenda for a discussion with the president about a program for rural economic development in Kennedy's second term in office.

The meeting occurred in August 1963. The secretary asked the president to broaden the USDA's mission, recognizing that no design existed for a management system that could identify resource needs in rural areas while ensuring their availability. He said the trends in farm income would inexorably lead more farmers and most rural residents to rely on off-farm income, a pattern already evident in every agricultural community. Supply management could sustain the highly productive core of agriculture and ensure stable food supplies, Freeman argued, but the policy emphasis had to shift to creating more pillars of growth in rural counties and cities. A rural economy built around agriculture and farming alone would continue to shrink.

Kennedy and Freeman were optimistic. They shared the belief that the president would win reelection in 1964 and govern for another four years. They agreed Congress likely would adopt supply management as the basic U.S. farm policy after the election. And a permanent food stamp program would be adopted, eliminating hunger as a chronic condition afflicting low-income families and individuals. Kennedy agreed Freeman should focus on building rural infrastructure and a new development architecture for the rural economy, expanding the mission of the USDA.

Three months later an assassin's bullet killed President Kennedy in Dallas.

Cabinet members returning to Washington after the assassination (l-r): White House Press Secretary Pierre Salinger, Secretary Freeman, Secretary of the Treasury Douglas Dillon, Secretary of State Dean Rusk, Secretary of the Interior Stuart Udall, Secretary of Commerce Luther Hodges, Chair of the Council of Economic Advisers Walter Heller, and Secretary of Labor Willard Wirtz

5

President Kennedy Is Dead
A First-Hand Account

The assassination of President John F. Kennedy on November 22, 1963, was a traumatic event for all Americans, especially for his cabinet members; almost all of them spent the horrendous day confined together in an airplane over the Pacific Ocean. They were flying to a diplomatic meeting in Tokyo with counterparts in the Japanese government. In retrospect, the trip was a questionable decision exposing the American government to the loss of its top leadership should the plane crash.

Countless books have been written about President Kennedy and the events of the days of mourning that followed his tragic death. Until now, however, none has given American readers an up-close, intimate account of the loss, grief, confusion, and resolution of the group of American leaders President Kennedy had selected to govern with him.

Secretary Freeman recounted in his personal diary the events that followed the cabinet's learning of Kennedy's death. Fifty years later, his words create a sense of sorrow and a struggle to cope, of grasping the responsibility for leadership entrusted to those the president had chosen:

November 23, 1963, 5:15 PM: I want to dictate the frightful events of the past several days:

November 21,1963, last Thursday: Jane and I went to the airport. She and I were up late packing, and I wasn't feeling too hot. We piled on the big jet, and it was a gay group heading for meeting in Tokyo with our counterparts in the Japanese government. After a brief oversight layover in Hawaii, the plane left Honolulu.

November 22, 1963, bound for Tokyo: Around 9 AM, about an hour after our departure, I noted my cabinet colleagues going forward into a compartment where Dean Rusk [secretary of state] and Doug Dillon [secretary of the treasury] were seated. Bob Manning, the press man from the State Department, came for me. He was sober, but I didn't think too much about it because I figured they were going to have something of a staff conference. He took my breakfast tray, and I squeezed by Jane and opened the door. There was a mood of great seriousness. The thought flashed into my mind that maybe something [had] happened in Japan so we [couldn't] go. Then someone said, "President Kennedy has been assassinated in Dallas. They don't know if he is dead or not. Governor Connally [of Texas] was also shot."

There were conflicting cables, and I looked them over. One said President Kennedy was dead, quoting a secret service man. Another said he was seriously wounded and that he was receiving a blood transfusion. So far these were not positively confirmed. We could make no direct contact. So Dean Rusk asked if we should turn back, and we all agreed we should. And we did, without waiting for definite confirmation.

The messages began to come in quickly, and we discussed what to do. First, Rusk said that he was going to go back to Hawaii, pick up a special plane, and go to Dallas. I asked him why, and he didn't have [an answer except something about] the secretary of state participating at the swearing in and concerns about who had his finger on the nuclear button.

I asked Rusk, and he said there was a letter from JFK to LBJ in event of a temporary disability. So Rusk was going to Dallas. People were desperately trying to make phone connections, and Rusk did reach Ball [George Ball, undersecretary of state for economic and agricultural affairs], and Ball's information was no more than ours: not clear whether the injury was fatal or only serious.

We sat around not knowing what to do or say, and the word came that we should all return to Washington. Rusk asked the very obvious question, "Who said so? Who is in Washington?" Nobody seemed to know who had sent word.

Then information came that Connally was in the operating room. There was a ray of hope. I grimly pointed out that I was walking proof that a man could get shot in the head and still live and told them where the bullet went through me.[1]

And so we waited.

Then came final confirmation. Dean Rusk said over the airplane intercom: "Ladies and gentlemen, this is the secretary of state. I deeply regret to inform you that the president is dead. May God help our country." There was complete silence. Some sobbing and tears. Very strange. A strained atmosphere.

Jane took my hand, the bad one, and squeezed it so hard that it hurt and said, "Poor Jackie."

Then she said to me, "I'm so glad you were not named vice president in Los Angeles. I'm too selfish."[2]

The thought had been in my mind, too. How different it might have been, but who knows? The hand of fate draws the picture.

Thank goodness President Johnson has had magnificent training these last three years, but he does not have this sense of the time and the age and the forces that John F. Kennedy had to such an unusual degree. It's odd. Dick Goodwin [one of the president's speechwriters] said in the White House today that Jack Kennedy was never really outgoing in the sense that people felt close to him . . . yet he had that peculiar quality that so endeared him and commanded such loyalty and devotion.

And Frank Roosevelt [son of President Franklin D. Roosevelt], who was sitting there at the time, said, "It's always been that way. We were kids in school together. He had this quality [that] even his brother (who was killed in the war and was supposed to be the No. 1 Kennedy) didn't have like Jack did."

I must say that I never had a real feeling of closeness to him as a person, much less than I have right now with President Johnson. But yet that quality was there so you could almost say that you love that man. I remember how he teased me on a trip about writing a book . . . how he teased me about four-hour speeches, and how in little ways sometimes my strong advocacy and vigorous espousal of causes seemed to impress him but were so different from his somewhat taciturn New England attitudes that I sometimes felt that he was a little bit uncomfortable.

Yet when I turned loose in Cabinet meetings, or when

I took a firm position on something he always said OK and backed me up. Other cabinet officers by and large said the same thing. Dillon said he had the same experience and what a marvelous and wonderful man Kennedy was to work for. Then something interesting came out, apparently from Phyllis Dillon—who was really sweet to Jane—to the effect that when Dillon was appointed, this meant to them something that they had earned on their abilities for he, Dillon, had always contributed to the other party.

Jane and I visited en route on the plane, and she expressed her affection for this great man now gone. She said there was a growing sense of progress and purpose and direction. We were making progress. There was enlightenment. What a crime that he must be gone. We would have won the election in '64. He had a wonderful reception in Dallas. We could have gone forward with the progress to abolish poverty and to spread freedom. With an election mandate beyond him and the years of experience and energy and the ability and affection, he could have moved the country, but somehow God saw otherwise.

There was a lot of discussion about how LBJ will do. [Secretary of the Interior Stuart] Udall and I were the only ones who really knew him. The Hodgeses are a little cool, and Luther [Hodges, secretary of commerce] said the South, particularly Texas, hated Lyndon because he was a traitor. When I pushed him, he acknowledged that it was mostly businessmen that he had talked to. Udall was a Johnson partisan and said he had supported him strongly for vice president. He felt that he would be a strong president. Wirtz [W. Willard (Bill) Wirtz, secretary of labor], didn't know.

I was pleased to learn that Lyndon had been briefed every day by a State Department guy on the cables that came in and was alerted as to events around the world. He was generally, I think, pretty deeply involved in most things that went on—except the economics. The question of tax cuts and its merits, the balance of payments—these economic questions he did not know and had little interest in them. This was confirmed when he said to me today in our little conference that he really didn't know what the implications of the tax cut meant and how important it was.

So here is an area, indeed, where he had a blank spot, and I had a chance to give Walter Heller [head of the Council of Economic Advisers and former economic adviser to Governor Freeman] a plug, which I hoped registered.

I said in these discussions about LBJ that men rise to the occasion, and this is a strong, take-charge man. But what a different place the White House will be. I suppose Jane and I have better relations with Lady Bird and Lyndon than anyone in the cabinet. He is a kind of old agrarian populist. Hard to tell what he will do.

The airplane was being refueled in Hawaii for the return flight to Washington. I laid back and put a handkerchief under my glasses and had a kind of little private cry, and then I pictured President Kennedy as I last called on him on Wednesday noon and gave my report on Western Europe, the Mansholt Plan, the EEC [European Economic Community, or Common Market], and what it meant.

As I went over it and how our interests were questioned, he said incisively, "Well, if they are unwilling to cooperate with us, we don't have to have a Kennedy Round [sixth session of General Agreement on Tariffs and Trade negotiations]. This Common Market may have been oversold anyway." We left it at that, but he looked so good.

November 23, 1963: We arrived back in Washington, at 1 am

Jane and I sat and talked almost until morning light, and with only a few hours' sleep, I came to the office this morning.

We went to the White House, where we assembled in the Cabinet Room. Mike Freeman [Orville and Jane's son, later a state senator, gubernatorial candidate, and longtime Hennepin County Attorney] was with us. We then walked over under the portico by the Rose Garden, through the doorway to the swimming pool, down the hall in the White House on the East side, up the steps, and into the Rose Room, where we waited with congressional leaders and then filed into the East Room.

Jane said to me, "What an improvement in this place by the Kennedys since we first came."

The caisson was elevated in a kind of podium; around it there were some [kneelers] for people who wished to kneel and pray. There was one big spray of flowers, otherwise very plain and dignified. The casket was closed.

The spirit of the man was everywhere. We went to the West Entrance, where I always go, and Jane and Mike followed me up the stairs by Ted Sorenson's [Kennedy's senior counselor and chief speechwriter] office, by Ken O'Donnell's [chief of staff] office and into the Cabinet Room, where most of the cabinet had assembled. It was almost like the end of the trail—it will never seem the same.

I walked into Mrs. Lincoln's [Evelyn Norton, the president's personal secretary] office, which was being rapidly changed over, and into the president's office, where they were moving out his things. The desk, always cluttered with pictures and pieces of ivory and all kinds of gadgets, so much so that I often marveled how he could possibly work on it, was now clean. The partition in the front of the ancient desk that they dug out of the basement of the White House when he first took office, and [that] *Look* magazine last week emphasized as a hiding place for John-John, was partially slid back. The ships that he loved (and that were displayed around the room) were now piled in one corner.

When we came back from viewing the caisson, the room was almost totally bare. I said to Jane, "It'll never be the same."

She said, "That's true, but we must go forward. It won't be the same; it never could be."

We came back to the department and had a cup of coffee. Mike told me that he got cut yesterday from the basketball team. Poor boy, that's really a heartbreak and a loss. He took it bravely and said he was going to play on the church team, and I told him I got cut of the basketball team in high school, too, and would not have been in football except [that] they didn't cut. People just quit. That I finally got there, and this is [where] they separate the men from the boys. This meant so much to him. He needs his dad a bit more on some of these things. A hard go.

Jane and Mike went home, and I got Charlie Murphy [undersecretary of agriculture] and Charles Grant [director of the USDA Office of Budget and Finance] in and went over the budget because I thought we would discuss in the Cabinet meeting the president's possible message—the new president, that is—and the tax, finance, budget, and politics of it might be very pertinent.

Back I went to the White House after getting the figures clearly in mind and having a quick cheeseburger. We gathered and stood around talking quietly. The new president came in, and Dean Rusk said, "Gentlemen, the president of the United States." We stood up.

He opened the meeting with a testimonial to President Kennedy, said he wanted to keep us all and that he needed us, that we had great responsibilities. He had already started when Bobby Kennedy [the president's brother and attorney general] came in. Somebody got up, others did not, so some were up and some were not. President Johnson was not.

Bobby sat down. He said nothing. When President Johnson finished, Dean pledged his devotion and that of all of us serving him. Adlai Stevenson [U.S. Ambassador to the UN] did the same, citing his seniority in a sense and saying that he had made a pledge of loyalty to President Kennedy and so he would make one now to President Johnson. With that, the meeting was over.

We all stood around, frustrated, not knowing what to do, because the occasion and the situation it reflected were obviously most unsatisfactory. President Johnson said he would address a joint session of Congress on Wednesday. On the plane yesterday, and in our quiet discussions during the day, most of the cabinet has felt that he ought to speak to the country at large and then perhaps to the Congress, but that the country would look for a word from him promptly.

President Johnson was talking in a corner a bit with Dean Rusk and then with Ted Sorenson, apparently asking Ted to write something, for he had said to each of us [that] he would like to have from us some recommendations in hand by the end of Monday. I didn't know what to do because I felt that this first message was so important and that this domestic economy question needed to be faced and that budget cutting was not necessarily good politics at all.

I hesitated to burden him but walked around the table, and when he was detached for a moment, I grabbed him by the shoulder and said: "There are some important things about this that ought to be discussed before you deliver your message."

"Well," he said, "I don't know about the funeral; I may be in Massachusetts on Tuesday. Give me a call and see about coming in Monday." That answer was highly unsatisfactory. He also said that members of Congress, not mentioning names, were petitioning him in terms of the economy. I didn't know what to do and stood around. Finally, he left.

I went out in the corridor and walked down the same familiar route. Then I stopped and came back. I went into a little room where Dick Goodwin [speechwriter and counselor to the president] and Bob McNamara [secretary of defense] were talking; McNamara was making the arrangements for the funeral, which apparently will include a resting place in Arlington.

I went to see Ted Sorensen and tried to talk a bit with him, but he was in a state of shock. He said that he had invested 10 years in this man who was suddenly gone, whom he loved so much and who meant so much. He said he wanted to do his best, but he didn't know whether he would stay or could work. I tried to talk to him about the difference of the situation now and what ought to be written. I gave him some material, but he just wasn't there.

There were tears in his eyes and mine. I reminded him that I became a Kennedy partisan on the day long ago when Sorensen came to the 1960 Minnesota DFL convention, and . . . he came out to our house as the dawn was breaking and Jane made us a cup of coffee. How well I remember that. He did, too, and I said to him. "We've traveled a long road since then."[3]

Ted clearly was lost in his thoughts, so I left to go to the Old Executive Office Building across the West Wing to find President Johnson's temporary office. I ran into Ken Galbraith, who grabbed me and said, "You're the most important guy in the whole business. You stay put; he really needs you . . . We've got to take care of some of these liberals now so they don't go shooting off their mouth. Johnson has to be elected president."

Galbraith said he was busy drafting a speech. That was encouraging. I asked him if I should go and see Johnson and he said yes. So I walked into the Old Executive Office Building, found out where Johnson was, walked through the Press, went up in the elevator, walked into Johnson's office, sat down, and received a warm welcome from Cliff Carter [longtime Johnson staff aide].

It wasn't until 10 minutes before I was ushered in. It was a different Lyndon Johnson than I had seen over the past three years. Actually the frustration seemed gone; he seemed relaxed; the power, the confidence, and the assurance of Majority Leader Lyndon Johnson seemed to be there. He had placed a call to labor leaders, and he talked with Alec Rose [Garment Workers Union leader] in a very relaxed and friendly way, asking for his help.

I then talked to him about what concerned me and told him that the cabinet felt that he really should speak to the people and then to the joint session of Congress. Then he told me that he had real problems with the family. I guess that means Bobby. He said that when the plane came in [to fly Johnson and the body of President Kennedy back to Washington], despite the fact that Johnson held the plane in Dallas for an hour and a half waiting for Mrs. Kennedy and the president's body . . . when the plane came in Bobby met with the family, that they paid no attention to Johnson whatever, that they took the body off the plane, put it in the hearse, took Mrs. Kennedy along, and departed.

Only then did Johnson leave the plane—without any attention directed or any courtesy toward him as the president of the United States. But Johnson said that he just turned the other cheek. Apparently, he said, Bobby's late entrance into the Cabinet Room was purposeful, and . . . Bobby had said to an aide that we won't go in until he has already sat down.

There was bitterness in Lyndon's voice on this one, and he asked. "What can I do? I do not want to get into a fight with the family, and the aura of Kennedy is important to all of us."

Therefore, Johnson hesitates to speak to the people, which I think he should. And therefore, he delays in speaking to the Congress, which I think he shouldn't. Apparently the Congress, some of them at least—and he even cited Senator Humphrey—said they wanted to recess and go home, that they were getting nowhere.

President Johnson said if they did not go along with his recommendation for a joint session, we would start out being repudiated, and we had to do something about Congress and the miserable state it was in now. He did not want to be repudiated by them, but if he had to wait until Wednesday, it would be too late, and many of them would already be gone. And so he is in something of a conundrum.

I made my pitch quite clear that he ought not to get too involved as a moderate or relative conservative, and he certainly ought to be careful in this first speech because liberals were the ones he would find hard to reach. They might start shooting with his first message, as distinguished from President Kennedy, who had strong liberal support and was playing for the middle of the road. He was relatively noncommittal on this, but overall was very, very, friendly.

President Johnson saw me to the door, and he was told Sargent Shriver [brother-in-law of President Kennedy, first director of the Peace Corps] was there to see him. President Johnson was clearly anxious to meet the family.

This attitude confirmed what Luther Hodges said on the plane, that at some recent meeting of the Kennedy family, Bobby had strongly attacked Lyndon. This would tend to confirm rumors that Bobby was doing so around town following the Bobby Baker matter, but that Jackie Kennedy had climbed all over Bobby, saying she wouldn't listen to this, that Lyndon had been kind, helpful, and loyal, and this just wasn't fair. She wouldn't tolerate it or listen to it.[4]

Luther Hodges had said that this was reported to him by a person who wasn't there. Lyndon said himself that Jackie had been just great, that she had said she would move out as soon as she could, and he had told her, "Honey, you stay as long as you want. I have a nice comfortable house, and I'm in no hurry. You have a tragedy and many problems."

Apparently that dear girl hardly went to bed and stayed with the body at the hospital [when President Kennedy's body was examined at Bethesda Naval Hospital]. When McNamara went out to check late last night, he found her still up and talking, and so he called Margy [Margaret Craig] McNamara, who came out and spent most of the night talking with Mrs. Kennedy. Then she brought the body to the White House and arranged it, refusing any kind of sedation. She was apparently sleeping in the White House this afternoon. God protect her; she sure has a lot of courage. What a lively girl and what a loss. Apparently she also took the children in to see the caisson—what a tragedy.

I returned to the office determined that we would do something, and I subsequently called Bill Wirtz, who was crushed. He said today was worse than yesterday and that the cabinet meeting was so awful. I hinted to him that it was awful because Lyndon felt he couldn't do anything because anything he did would be resented by the family, and as [Lyndon] responded when I told [him] that we had all felt that he ought to speak first to the people, then the Congress, he would not do that because the family would resent it and he would not get into any disagreement publicly with the family. So that took care of that.

I hinted at this with Wirtz, and he felt better. I told him that we ought to get something written, and he felt better. He promised to put a man on it, and we'll meet tomorrow afternoon in my office to go over some language.

Then I got hold of Udall, and he will do the same. Then I got hold of Dorothy Jacobson [Freeman's longtime adviser and chief speechwriter], and she will prepare something for me. Then I talked to Ken Galbraith at great length and got some material prepared to send over to him. He said he would be happy to be at the meeting too.

This all needs to be coordinated, but it presents a posture that does not foreclose the public investment route and counteracts Lyndon Johnson being labeled as a rank conservative in his first step out. I hope these matters might be thrashed out in a cabinet meeting, but I did call Walter Jenkins [Johnson's chief of staff], and told him what I was doing and that we were trying to put something in his hands, that there were two schools of thought on this [the question of public versus private investment in public services], that as between Walter Heller [chief of the Council of Economic Advisers] and Doug Dillon that Heller was the one to follow.

I then talked to Walter, told him he ought to go see Lyndon Johnson. He was going to do so later today, and he felt much better because of it. There is a vacuum here, and I'm trying to move in and do something about it. What a depressing day, but life must go on.

Top: Secretary Freeman was a city boy who learned to milk a cow on his grandfather's farm. Above: President Lyndon B. Johnson hands signing pens to Secretary Freeman, Sen. George Aiken (R-VT), Rep. Leonor K. Sullivan (D-MO), and Rep. Harold Cooley (D-NC) after signing the Food Stamp Act on August 31, 1964.

6

Protecting the Consumer

Freeman shared the commitment of Presidents Kennedy and Johnson to protect consumers. Product standards for conventional meat food products in 1960 were set through rules for field operations in regulatory directives to regional offices. This procedure indirectly incorporated product standards that essentially reflected industry practices limited by the cultural conventions of consumers. Food processors' attempts to manipulate conventional product content that changed the outward appearance of meat products or altered cultural expectations generally failed. This was early in the days of marketing methods designed in accordance with information distilled by individuals over centuries to protect against merchants of fraud.

The introduction of science and technology to food and agriculture overcame that problem for the industry. Long-term cultural practices were identified, then manipulated and exploited to encourage public acceptance while social costs were largely ignored. Science provided the food industry with immediate financial benefit through the manipulation of product content and exploitation through deception, though only if the government colluded with industry goals by failing to protect the public from the economic and physical costs of that deception.

The Eisenhower administration had approved an industry proposal to permit the sale of hams containing unlimited amounts of water, modifying regulatory controls in the Department of Agriculture on traditional practice in curing ham. Before the change, the USDA's meat inspection service required meatpackers and other processors to market hams sold in interstate commerce at no more than green weight—that is, at no more than they were before curing. Processors made ham through two conventional methods. One was the traditional country cure of burying fresh pork, or "green" ham, in salt, an ancient technology driving out all moisture and leaving a shriveled product that could be stored indefinitely but reconstituted by a long soaking in water. The other was a process infusing the green ham with a curing solution that increased the normal weight by as much as 50 percent. Shortly after Freeman became secretary, consumer complaints that their baking pans were full of water after cooking hams began flooding the USDA. They said the hams they bought were leaky, not dry to the touch.

Curing by infusion was used when ham was a food product made by myriad local producers whose businesses depended on a reputation for quality and honesty, one often supporting a family tradition and business. The local butcher who also made hams did not survive for long if the women who did the shopping and cooked the family meal noticed that the hams of a particular butcher always left more water in the baking pan than those of others. The news circulated quickly at local church events and elsewhere, and eventually the community or neighborhood had one less butcher.

Why were consumers complaining to the secretary of agriculture? Mostly because they were buying ham in supermarkets rather than from local butchers. Ham was no longer a local food product. The meatpacking business was undergoing consolidation, and supermarket chains were creating marketing systems that bought food products, especially processed meat such as ham, from distant corporations operating multiple plants in dozens of states supplying regional and national retail markets.

The local butcher was disappearing, and the consumer had to depend on package labels for the precautionary news once spread by word of mouth. The labels were billboards extolling the company's virtues, and they couldn't be trusted. Secretaries of agriculture had traditionally touted the USDA as protecting consumers by inspecting all meat and meat food products and removing contaminated and unfit products. Consumers who wanted neither excessive water nor unfit food had nowhere to go to protect their pocketbooks other than to ask the secretary for help with leaky ham.

By fortune if not coincidence, consumers were asking for help from the one person in Washington who understood the meat industry. Before his appointment as secretary of agriculture, Freeman had served three terms as the governor of Minnesota. In 1959 he was in a no-holds-barred confrontation with Wilson and Company, then a major U.S. meatpacking firm, headquartered in Chicago and operating a meatpacking plant in Albert Lea, Minnesota.

Wilson had sited the Albert Lea plant in an adjacent township, a local government entity created by state legislatures to conduct public business affecting property in the absence of other governmental bodies such as villages, towns, and cities. Wilson had fought successfully to exclude the township from incorporation into Albert Lea. After World War II, the city was expanding to provide housing, public services such as utilities, fire and police protection, hospitals, schools, and water, sewage and other environmental services for a growing middle class of families, many of them working at the Wilson plant. The company contracted with the City of Albert Lea to provide fire and police protection and aggressively opposed efforts of city government to control pollution of a big lake adjacent to Albert Lea and the township.

Wilson polluted the lake by dumping packing waste into it but paid no local taxes to ensure environmental quality.

Wilson also had bitterly fought unions established by workers to protect jobs and wages, and the company agreed to negotiate those issues only after Congress adopted laws during the Roosevelt administration recognizing collective bargaining as a right of American workers. In 1959 Wilson had adopted tactics indicating a fundamental change in company policy on labor and community relations. Wilson withdrew from an industry representing all meatpacking companies that negotiated industry-wide terms for wages and working standards.

Wilson presented the union representing Albert Lea workers with a contract it said was not negotiable. The union requested meetings for collective bargaining, but the company refused, agreeing only to a short-term extension of the existing contract. As the stalemate continued, Wilson contracted to recruit nonunion workers, threatening to replace union members. Repeating the union request for collective bargaining, workers also began planning to counter Wilson by voting to authorize the union to organize a picket line. Wilson raised the tension by announcing it would hire nonunion workers, and workers countered by voting to authorize a strike, charging that Wilson was in violation of federal law by refusing to bargain.

Wilson pushed the confrontation further by announcing it would hire replacement workers, an action to which the workers responded by picketing the plant. In effect, Wilson was raising the level of conflict by hiring nonunion workers to replace striking union workers. Wilson was now threatening the community, demanding that families living as neighbors for generations decide whether they would support the company or their neighbors who worked at the Wilson plant and were union members. Although other packing companies had negotiated new contracts with unions representing workers, Wilson refused. The company began hiring nonunion workers to break the strike.

The first nonunion workers drove through the union picket lines in mid-December 1959, creating an unbearable level of tension at the plant and within the community. Wilson asked Albert Lea police to protect access to the plant and requested local courts to restrain union efforts, calling picketing an illegal action to prevent access to its plant.

Closely monitoring the labor-management dispute, Governor Freeman offered the services of state government mediators, urged Wilson to follow the federal law on collective bargaining, and counseled union leaders to prevent violence on the picket lines. Wilson management, more than any other business leaders, knew that meatpacking is an industry that employs violence as a business practice—that is, it pays employees to slaughter cattle and hogs. Hiring replacement workers had the propensity to escalate tensions, which led to a striking worker injuring a replacement worker crossing the picket line.

Before the plant could open the next day, Governor Freeman ordered the Minnesota National Guard to close the plant so as to prevent further violence and protect public safety. The action came as a total surprise, mainly because military force by state government had largely been used to protect private property rights over the public interest. The business community was outraged. Editorial pages denounced Freeman across the United States.

Wilson immediately sued the governor of Minnesota, claiming Freeman had exceeded his authority by denying the company the use of its private property, asking the federal courts to compel the governor to protect the company. Wilson's legal advisers, mindful that the company had initiated the confrontation and was in violation of the federal law to recognize collective bargaining, apparently advised Wilson management to come to the bargaining table before the court case began.

Almost 25 years earlier, a similar three-judge panel had faced the same situation when Gov. Floyd B. Olson declared martial law in Minneapolis after workers engaged in bloody combat with police and businessmen over work issues. A business coalition sued Governor Olson to lift martial law. With both labor and business ready to resume the strife, the courts discreetly left the issue to the constitutional authority of Governor Olson.

Several days before a three-judge federal court panel began hearing arguments on the litigation against Governor Freeman, Wilson announced the company would begin collective bargaining with the workers' union. The federal panel criticized the decision by Freeman to close the Wilson plant but offered no judicial standards to restrict the constitutional powers of Minnesota governors. The panel said the questions leading to closing the plant were by then moot in view of the continuing collective bargaining over wages and working standards between the company and the workers' union. That is, the reasons for closing the plant no longer existed.

In view of these facts, the panel ordered Governor Freeman to send home the National Guard, allowing Wilson to resume plant operation. Freeman withdrew the National Guard troops, noting that by dropping its refusal to bargain with the workers union, the company had acknowledged its complicity, ending the labor-management clash that triggered the strike. The company insisted it would honor Wilson's promises of permanent employment for workers hired to break the strike. But Wilson also said the issue would be resolved at the bargaining table. Subsequently the company agreed to restore union-member workers to seniority positions and retain the longevity privileges they held before the strike.

The message to Albert Lea from the federal court system was that worker rights in the absence of strong support from the executive branch were in jeopardy. Still, it warned, should corporate interests confront the constitutional authority of the executive, they shouldn't expect help.

Later, in Washington, Freeman did not wait long to dewater the Eisenhower ham, telling the meat industry that the green-weight rule was to be enforced. Angry that its deception had been exposed, the leaders charged Freeman with threatening the free enterprise system and capitalism. They sued the secretary in federal court, insisting that their economic interests had been injured and pleading that they were only doing what the Eisenhower administration said was legal.

The federal court used the litigation to prescribe a product standard for hams and a standard for labeling hams. In its wisdom, the court said a ham containing 10 percent or less additional water could be identified on its label as *ham* in big typeface while accompanied by warning in the ingredient panel that the ham had water added. Ham containing up to 30 percent water by weight was required to carry a label including the words *added water* in a typeface only slightly smaller, near the word *ham*. In effect, the court warned the secretary to let in a little water. The ruling implied that the harm to the consumer pocketbook would not be noticeable, and it ignored any nutritional consequences.

Another consumer issue was that of added fat. The USDA learned of the problem when consumers began using cynical humor to complain that hot dogs were mislabeled. The cynics argued that people should stick a wick in some hot dogs and call them candles—the product was more fat than it was meat.

Hot dogs are uniquely an American sausage, a meat food product that, seasoned to taste with salt, nitrates, and other preservatives, is a way to tastily package the remnants of cattle, hogs, and other animals trimmed from carcasses during processing. Ingredients are always a matter of conjecture. Otto von Bismarck, the German politician credited with organizing the modern German state, famously remarked that people should never ask how sausages or laws are made.

Before World War II, hot dogs with more than 17 percent fat by content felt greasy and had a poor taste. Consumers rejected them.

After World War II, scientists triumphantly created a process enabling the meat-processing industry to manipulate the content of hot dogs. Trimmings became the ingredients for a colloid substance in which tiny fat globules were encased in microscopically thin protein membranes, and the fat content of hot dogs or other sausages could be raised to nearly 75 percent without visibly altering the product. At room temperature the "new" hot dog looks like a solid product, pinkish in color, firm to the touch, chewable, and tastily modeled to the preferences of test audiences. Best of all, for meatpackers, fat content could be more than doubled, allowing fat to replace meat that cost three to four times as much at wholesale.

The only problem was that the colloid hot dog was, in fact, a liquid that, when heated, broke down into visibly distinct components of fat and protein. Cooked in hot water, the fat to protein content of the modern hot dog was visible for everyone to see. And what American consumers saw did *not* please them, especially when the liquid fat content was the greater part of their hot dogs. They complained to Secretary Freeman, saying the hot dog wasn't what it seemed.

About the same time, water in lakes and streams across the United States was foaming bubbles from chemicals in soap detergents that sewage systems could not remove. Rivers burst into flames from contaminants. New automobiles driven on the not-yet-completed interstate system crashed into the medians. Farm chemicals for killing pests entered the ecosystem, thinning the shells of eggs of wild eagles, threatening their extinction. And hot dogs—as appealing as Snow White's apple before one bit into them—were not what people thought they saw.

The beef generally used in making hot dogs came from older cattle, typically milk cows at the end of their productive lives. The meat was stringy, tough, good for stews, and about 18 percent fat. Secretary Freeman had no official content standards for hot dogs as a guide. His authority to set standards relied on the Meat Inspection Act adopted in 1906, authorizing the president to define the term *wholesome* as the standard for meat that could be shipped in interstate commerce—that is, across state lines. The statute delegates the authority to the secretary of agriculture. A half-century after the act went into effect, he was asked, "What is a hot dog? Is it wholesome?"

Secretary Freeman concluded that after 50 years of existence, no one could doubt the hot dog was a wholesome meat food product, that it could be recognized as generally a safe food when made from meat inspected and approved by federal inspectors. And hot dogs made in federally inspected plants could be shipped across state lines, he said, if they contained no added fat—that is, no more than the average fat content of beef typically used in making hot dogs, or 18 percent. Meatpackers—once more embarrassed that Freeman had caught them in a public deception and angry that a federal official had the temerity to tell industry executives the limits of their discretion —were outraged. The meatpacking industry sued the secretary in federal court.

The court faced a dilemma. The industry action could not pass the laugh test—that is, no person could say with a straight face that a product with a fat content of 70 percent was a hot dog. At the same time, Secretary Freeman had carved out a strong, logical argument based on facts beyond question. He was neither arbitrary nor capricious, and he had not exceeded his authority. Nothing in the statute, however, tied the court's hands. Congress had not explicitly authorized Freeman to say how much fat should be in a manufactured food product. Neither had Congress specified how that decision should be made.

The occasion was a Solomonic opportunity, and the federal judge cut the baby in half. In the court's judgment the proper amount of fat in America's hot dog was somewhere between the plaintiff's and the defendant's preferences, and about 28 percent was just right. Thus, an American hot dog may contain no more than 28 percent fat. This decision satisfied no one.

From a larger perspective, the question was how to focus priorities on issues of governance while recognizing irresponsible corporate behavior as essentially an issue of procedure and administrative process.

The Administrative Procedures Act (APA, 1946) was enlarged to establish a process to authorize the executive branch to develop rules of corporate behavior, including product standards, in which the authority of the executive branch was tightly constrained. The executive could act in the public interest so long as the federal courts did not perceive the action as arbitrary or capricious.

In general, an "arbitrary" executive fails to establish and follow procedure to determine the public interest in an issue such as through holding public hearings to allow for interested parties to present relevant information and evidence. A "capricious" executive fails to demonstrate to the courts that its action is based on relevant scientific data and evidence. In practice, the constraints on arbitrary and capricious actions are largely directed at the federal civil service bureaucracy because it likely initiates regulatory actions while operating in the interest of the executive branch (the president and those appointed by the president).

The task for Secretary Freeman was not only to introduce new rule-making procedures in USDA programs but also to strengthen and reorganize its major consumer programs, particularly those involving food safety.

The problem in fact was the failure of the state inspection programs going back to 1906, when Congress made meat inspection a federal service. Federal inspection was authorized for meat and meat foods sold in interstate commerce, primarily to cope with the misbehavior of slaughter and processing corporations in Chicago and Kansas City (the Beef Trust). Smaller slaughter and processing establishments selling to nearby markets were the responsibility of state and city inspection programs, mostly nonexistent as the 20th century began. By 1960, however, particularly with the rise of big urban population centers served by slaughter and processing within state borders, state inspection programs had begun handling larger volumes of meat processing, creating competing inspection services of unequal quality.

If a cattle buyer had an inventory of animals including diseased cows—which was fairly common—a federal inspection was more likely than a state inspection to result in the condemnation of unfit animals. Inspection is primarily a matter of budgets and economics, with state inspection programs more likely to be underfunded and understaffed than federal inspection services.

Further, the standards for program operations varied from one state program to the next, and federal inspection standard deviations varied from one region to the next because office supervisors were routinely rotated. As a result, cattle buyers tried to move unfit animals through state inspection programs, thus leaking a growing volume of unfit and unsafe meat into the nation's food supply.

The leak had to be sealed, but the program was a mix of political, territorial, organizational, and management issues. The federal government could not say publicly that a failure of state governments was putting consumers at risk. The secretary of agriculture could not say that 50 state legislatures were failing to adequately fund their meat inspection programs. Neither could he say the meat industry was complicit in allowing meat inspection programs to falter. Finally, it was administratively and politically infeasible for the USDA to offer training and other management programs to state inspection services so as to improve their operations.

All of these problems needed attention, but neither the president nor Congress could describe them publicly without setting off a raging controversy. To make matters worse, the meat inspection service, unbeknownst to Secretary Freeman, had quietly approached the leaders of House and Senate agriculture committees to explore legislative action, only to be met with stern warning not to stir up the wrath of the meat industry.

After rejecting a proposal from Secretary Freeman to deal with the matter, President Johnson agreed to ask Congress to amend the Meat Inspection Act. Freeman proposed that federal standards be the floor for meat inspection with any state free to adopt rules and regulation beyond the federal standard. The concept was, and is, unique. Industry and private corporations generally insist that federal standards preempt state laws and regulation. In this case, the federal government invited states to go further and offered them incentives to do so.

Industry prefers federal standards that legislatively preempt state regulations going further. Preemption of federal standards by state governments was one reason the meat industry opposed the legislation. State inspection officials joining the industry in opposing the legislation, both complaining that the Department of Agriculture should not be imposing federal standards on state government.

Industry also opposed another component of food safety reforms, that of requiring state inspection standards to equal federal standards. The proposed legislation would authorize the secretary to replace state inspection programs with federal inspection should state governments drop out of inspection services. Further, it would authorize the secretary to pay half the cost of revamped state programs should state legislatures continue the operation of state inspection services.

Ralph Nader, then at the height of his power as the nation's leading consumer advocate, vigorously supported the proposed food safety legislation. Unknowingly, he was a major lever in Freeman's success at gaining its passage. In addition to the public arguments that the USDA made in support of reforms, department officials prepared a "little black book" of photographs and descriptions of diseased animals awaiting slaughter and processing in state-inspected plants. USDA officials used the book as an exhibit during congressional visits to explain the problem that reform was intended to eliminate. It was an internal document meant for agency use in planning legislative changes.

Reporters learned of the little black book from sources in the congressional offices of senators and representatives supporting the legislation. They quickly informed Nader, who immediately demanded that the USDA release the book to the public. The meat industry recognized at once that the material would cause a scandal harmful to meat sales and the public image of the beef and pork industry. The department insisted the information was intended for internal management purposes, but industry and state government opposition to food safety reform legislation disappeared. Congress quickly enacted the legislation, amending the Meat Inspection Act the first and only time to date.

President Johnson, told earlier by his advisers not to expect passage of food safety legislation, was elated. A huge signing ceremony at the White House included the appearance of Upton Sinclair, a muckraking writer whose book *The Jungle* had exposed scandalous practices in slaughter plants 50 years earlier and prompted the original meat inspection act.

A year later, Congress amended the Poultry Products Inspection Act to include in poultry legislation the same criteria as in the Wholesome Meat Act. In the final action to rebuild the food safety management system in USDA, Secretary Freeman merged meat inspection with poultry inspection, creating a single inspection management structure. The poultry inspection program established in 1947 was a separate regulatory program with administrative staff duplicating that of meat inspection. The poultry industry, which viewed the separate agency mainly as a status symbol, strongly opposed the merger concept.

Industry lobbyists had prevailed upon Jamie Whitten, chair of the House Agriculture Subcommittee on Appropriations, to order the USDA not even to think about a merger. USDA officials quietly developed a cost analysis showing that the merger would produce $30 million in administrative savings over a single decade. After studying the analysis, Whitten ordered the USDA to implement the merger plans.

Taking a break from rafting on the Middle Fork of Salmon River. Chief of the U.S. Forest Service Ed Cliff stands directly behind the Freemans.

7

Defending the Land

Public Land and the Public Interest

Kennecott Copper Corporation in 1964 owned Miners Ridge, a giant parcel of land in the Glacier Peak Wilderness region of Montana, locked in the middle of the national forest system. The company believed huge deposits of copper and other metals were buried under the part of the forest it owned and wanted to dig an open-pit mine to strip out the Miners Ridge wealth.

Kennecott had one problem. Miners Ridge was surrounded by the Gore Range primitive forest area, a federal designation for remote areas such as those in the Glacier Peak national forests managed by the U.S. Forest Service (USFS). The company had purchased its isolated parcel of land from private owners who had no public right-of-way on which to build access roads. Kennecott could not get to Miners Ridge and its copper without federal help, particularly from the forest service.

87

The USFS is a major agency in the Department of Agriculture, assigned by President Theodore Roosevelt's executive order in the early years of the 20th century to shield the remaining American forests from the grasp of timber barons clear-cutting their way west through U.S. forests to the Pacific. Roosevelt expanded the management goals of public lands to include the public interest in preserving the wilderness, transferring the jurisdiction of forests from the Department of Interior but leaving mineral development management to Interior. This split in public management duties created a problem that fell into the lap of Secretary of Agriculture Orville L. Freeman in the form of access to Miners Ridge.

As governor of Minnesota, Freeman had vivid evidence of the environmental carnage of timber barons plundering through the state's great pine forests. The firestorm that destroyed Hinckley, Minnesota, in 1894, fueled by thousands of surrounding acres littered with branches and timber-cutting residue, killed hundreds of people. It was a horrific experience still remembered by Minnesotans in 1964.

Freeman also had fought U.S. Steel in the Minnesota legislature to get a fair price for the iron ore that the mining company dug out of the state's iron range, a massive deposit of iron ore stretching across northeastern Minnesota. And he had proposed funding of research programs at the University of Minnesota, where the process of concentrating low-grade ore into iron-rich taconite ore was developed, to preserve the economic future of the mining and steel industries after the high-grade iron ore was exhausted.

Secretary Freeman recognized that Kennecott, as an owner of private property surrounded by national forest, could ask for a right-of-way through public lands. The USDA's lawyers said the law was on the company's side. Freeman's instinct was to preserve, protect, and sustain resource for public uses. The thought of a raw wound as open, visible, and long lasting as an open-pit copper mine in the Gore Range—a vast primitive area in the Glacier Park forests—brought memories of the scars of open-pit mining on the Iron Range. But with the law on the company's side, Freeman's hands were tied.

Secretary Freeman told the Sierra Club, a national environmental preservation organization, that he hoped the application for Kennecott's right-of-way to Miners Ridge would never reach his desk. His choice of words left both the mining company and the environmentalists uncertain as to his action. The environmentalists hoped Freeman would reject the application, and the company feared he would, leaving it with a costly trail of lawsuits to pry its right from the federal government.

Kennecott's lawyers likely had given the company the same advice that the USDA lawyers carried to Secretary Freeman—that is, that the company had the law on its side. The USDA might delay approval of the right-of-way, but traditional practice and the weight of the law would prevail to further private over public interest. Nevertheless, the company had a greater burden to overcome in 1964 than it would have faced in earlier years.

Congress had adopted the Wilderness Act in 1964, legislation designating as wilderness the lands that previous secretaries of agriculture and the interior had earmarked as wilderness lands and forests. Development was prohibited, and public access was limited to hiking, horseback riding, canoeing, and rafting. Only Congress could change the designation of wilderness areas. The legislation also authorized the secretaries to manage "primitive areas" in the public interest. There were lands and forests not included in the wilderness areas definition.

When he became secretary, Freeman quickly signaled his responsibility to manage forests and public resources in the public interest in filling the position of chief forester. The secretary usually appoints the heads of USDA agencies from among the top agency managers, a practice encouraging stable process but also promoting policy inertia. New ideas and procedures tend to encounter difficulty as they percolate to the top in management. Sustainable management, before 1961, meant encouraging private development of forest resources as more consistent with the public interest than wilderness policies.

In selecting the chief forester in 1961, Freeman interviewed all the top candidates but reached several management levels below the conventional choices to select Ed Cliff, a longtime USDA forester whom Freeman found less hostile to the environmental management views that Congress incorporated in the Wilderness Act in 1964.

Kennecott interpreted Freeman's choice of Ed Cliff as providing the mining industry with more obstacles than encountered in past relations with the USFS. But the industry was resourceful: The new secretary might be cooler to mining industry goals than the companies preferred, but it was simply a problem that would take a bit of time to overcome. The question of access to the copper in Miners Ridge was a decision in which the secretaries of the Interior and of Transportation would have interest and input. If the companies could lead the secretaries and their departments to support the open-pit-mining enterprise, Freeman could not block it.

So the central issue was not whether Kennecott could develop the minerals but rather how the public interest would be defined in managing primitive wilderness areas in national forests. The Department of Transportation (DOT) was a party to the discussion in its role as builder of the massive federal highway system initiated by the Eisenhower administration in the 1950s. DOT was considering two possible routes for a section of Interstate 70 through the national forest of Glacier Peak.

One proposal called for a route bisecting the Gore Range primitive area and passing near Kennecott's Miners'Ridge property, with exit and entrance ramps for easy access to large-scale traffic from trucks hauling copper ore. The other called for a route skirting the primitive-area forests and leaving the wilderness largely untouched. The interstate highway system had priority over all other public-interest goals in the national government, leaving Freeman a choice between the two.

Predictably, after visits from Kennecott's lobbyists, the Department of Transportation engineers recommended to Secretary William Boyd that the department support the Interstate 70 route bisecting the Glacier Peak primitive forest area. The route skirting the Gore Range would be 10 miles longer. The route bisecting the forest was shorter and would be less expensive to construct. And since the interstate system was intended to increase economic growth as well as to improve transportation, the opportunity to exploit copper ore enhanced the potential benefits of the department's recommendation.

The staff of the Department of the Interior's Bureau of Mines was similarly impressed with the argument of Kennecott's lobbyists, and it recommended to Secretary Stuart Udall that it also support the open-pit mine proposed by Kennecott and endorse the DOT proposal to bisect the primitive area. Udall and Freeman shared similar and strongly held views on wilderness policy, but Udall as the secretary of the interior had to balance the views of the staff of the mineral development bureau with those of the wilderness area and National Park Service (NPS) staffs. On the Miners Ridge question, Udall's choice was not between private development and preserving the wilderness but rather whether to support or reject Freeman's choice between bisecting the primitive area and building the longer route circling the primitive wilderness . . .

Secretary Freeman prepared carefully for the showdown. Characteristically, he followed a well-established pattern that he had first developed as Minnesota's governor. He found an individual with background and expertise whom he could trust to research, compile, organize, and analyze the issue and provide a recommendation to guide his decision. Freeman detested kicking the can down the road. The secretary found his man in Bill Worf, a young agency forester who shared his views on preserving wilderness resources.

"I have the authority to act," the secretary explained, "but what is the public interest? What should I do? I don't want to intrude into the primitive wilderness if there is another option."

Freeman asked Worf to walk the two proposed routes for the Interstate 70 highway, one across Red Mountain and the other across Buffalo Mountain through Vail Pass, making careful observations and taking notes on comparative conditions and the likely consequences of disturbing or destroying the surroundings. The secretary said Worf should take as much time as he needed and report to Freeman upon his return.

After Worf returned to Washington, Secretary Freeman called a meeting in his USDA office to resolve the Interstate 70 issue. Secretary Udall and Secretary of Transportation Boyd were present, along with Ed Cliff and other members of the USFS staff, including Worf. Freeman asked Boyd to review the DOT proposal for a road bisecting the Gore Range primitive area through Vail Pass, the shortest and most direct route. After the presentation, Freeman asked Boyd whether his recommendation was the Vail Pass route, and Boyd agreed. Then Freeman asked Udall, who said he was presenting the recommendation of his mineral resource development group. Freeman did not ask Udall whether he was presenting the Interior Department's position.

Secretary Freeman then introduced Worf as his special assistant, explaining that Worf had been directed to walk the terrain of both options, and asked him to give his report to the group. Worf gave a detailed account of his observations and findings, noting the geographical differences between the two options and comparing the terrain and vegetation.

After asking Boyd and Udall whether they had any questions, Freeman turned to Worf and said, "You've heard the recommendations. I have the authority to act, but I'm asking what is the public interest? What should I do?"

"You have other options," Worf said.

Freeman paused, momentarily looking at Worf, then stared at the top of his desk. "You're goddam right," he said. "I have other options."

Then the Secretary Freeman turned to Boyd and said "Sorry, Boyd, you don't get the goddam road. You're going around—10 miles longer."

Udall smiled and said nothing.

The epilogue to the drama came 55 years later. Interstate 70 skirted the Glacier Peak Wilderness area. Kennecott did not apply for a permit to build an access road through national forests to the copper deposits of Miners Ridge. The land remained an undeveloped asset of the mining company, eventually passed to the bigger mining conglomerate that swallowed Kennecott. The forest service in 2009 traded other national forest lands for Miners Ridge, now officially included in the Gore Range primitive area of the service, a development briefly noted on the inner pages of just a few newspapers in the western United States. The primitive forest area is accessible on foot and horseback and is a great place to camp.

Introducing the concept of "other options" as a criterion for managing primitive areas in the wilderness system of national forests also brought closure to a policy dispute fracturing relations between the forest service and the park service for generations.

When President Teddy Roosevelt initially transferred jurisdiction of American public forests from the Department of the Interior to the USDA, he included national parks encompassed by national forests. Gifford Pinchot, a Pennsylvania forester appointed to lead the USFS, helped lead Roosevelt to make the shift. Pinchot adopted the concept of sustainable use to guide forest policy, a decision applauded by environmentalists. But the consensus was shattered when Pinchot endorsed a proposal by government officials of San Francisco and California to flood a canyon in Yosemite National Park, creating a water supply for the city.

John Muir, the iconic American naturalist who earlier led Roosevelt to create the national park system, denounced the proposal. Muir sought to preserve areas of unique natural beauty as the heritage of all Americans, and he bitterly opposed Pinchot's decision. The duel was resolved by President Woodrow Wilson when he authorized the flooding of the canyon as the San Francisco water source.

The dispute reflected a greater political controversy between sustainable use advocates and preservationists that led Congress in 1916 to create the National Park Service within the Department of the Interior. The action formally defined the preservation goals of the national park system and moved national park jurisdiction from the forest service.

Environmental policy evolved further in the 1960s with passage of the Wilderness Act, legislation that substantially increased the size and scope of the park service and greatly increased the area of national forests in which public uses are more broadly in play. Management policies became more complex, and Freeman's "other options" criteria became essential.

Rural Area Development

As the Department of Agriculture celebrated its centennial anniversary in 1963, Orville Freeman came to a startling conclusion. An abundance of food and fiber, symbol of the unparalleled success of American agriculture, was the product of a 100-year commitment of the government to a massive public interest of billions in agricultural research and financial support for farmers. It was a Janus bargain, however. In the rural America producing that abundance, people were living an economy resembling more that of a developing country than of the richest nation in the world.

Per capita income in rural America, compared to urban America, was significantly lower. Unemployment was higher, jobs were fewer, and lack of health services exposed people in rural communities to risk of premature death. Housing conditions were far worse than in urban areas, and children in rural schools were more likely to receive a poorer education.

Government policies have consequences, Freeman recognized—the problem was not the fault of farm policy but of the failure to understand the needs of rural America as more than farm policy. The rural economy needed more than agriculture could provide to sustain living standards comparable to those in urban areas. The economic gap between rural and urban America was expanding, but closing the gap would require new public programs and a sustained federal commitment to rural

America equal to that provided to agriculture a century earlier.

Freeman instinctively grasped the grim reality that rural America would experience 20 years later in the economic depression shaking the rural economy in the 1980s. If 600,000 farmers produced 85 to 90 percent of farm output in 1960, agriculture alone could not sustain the other 5 million farms—and the people living in towns and villages servicing the farms—in rural America. A crisis was approaching in the form of another agonizing shrinkage of the rural economy that would shatter the future for millions of men, women, and children. The loss of creativity and ingenuity would be even more devastating. It could be prevented through expansion of the rural economy—through rural area development.

As governor, Freeman had understood that failure to act would accelerate the gap between urban and rural life. The exodus of rural youth to find jobs and higher incomes in urban America would rob rural communities of future leadership. Consolidating school districts saved taxpayer dollars but shrank the rural economy and did not enrich education. Enticing corporations with tax benefits to bring factories to rural communities accelerated costs for water safety, sewage systems, and other infrastructure services. Migrations that earlier led black Americans in the South to travel north to urban centers and small farmers on the Great Plains to flee to the west while dust storms blew their farms east, transformed American culture but left rural America with an economy that collapsed from neglect, fear, and a loss of vision.

Rural area development was a concept for a new beginning, but a new beginning first required a plan. And Freeman had one. He also had an advantage few other Americans enjoyed: The secretary of agriculture could pick up the phone and call the president of the United States (POTUS) to discuss the plan, and the two could sit together and talk about the future.

Freeman called President Kennedy, and they met in the summer of 1962 to talk about rural area development. The men agreed that while much heavy lifting remained, their progress since 1961 in farm legislation and food policy had put the United States on the right side of history. Supply management policies could cap the uncontrollable rise in farm surpluses that led to steadily rising federal expenditures. The food stamp and child nutrition programs were the centerpieces of emerging food policy ensuring that economic status could not block access to an abundant food supply for Americans at risk of hunger and malnutrition.

Getting control of the cornucopia while providing every person with access to its bounty helped resolve two nagging policy issues and cleared the way for taking on an even more difficult public policy mission—building a new economy in rural America. Freeman asked President Kennedy to declare the mission of the Department of Agriculture during his second term as that of building a new rural economy. Kennedy said he was confident he would be reelected in 1964, a political outcome Freeman also believed was certain.

The secretary said the mission would have important political benefits, explaining that fewer than 10 percent of the 6 million farms counted in the most recent census produced nearly 90 percent of the nation's food. If 600,000 farms received most of the income from farming, then some 5.4 million farmers and farm families would need to find work and income off the farm simply to survive. Expanding the rural economy was important not only for farmers and farm families but also for millions of people working in rural communities providing services to farms and farm families.

Kennedy realistically had two options, Freeman said: Adopt the mission of building a new rural economy or permit the bleaker alternative of a economy dominated by larger and fewer farms supported by federal subsidies but with an unacceptable standard of living for many.[1] If federal programs are acceptable to help some groups in rural America, they should be acceptable to support the goals of all rural people, Freeman argued.

Explaining his plan for USDA's future mission, Secretary Freeman proposed an initial program of federal loans for building rural community infrastructure, primarily water and sewer systems in small towns and villages. Other suggested programs would improve rural communications, provide loans to assist individuals in building low-cost rural housing, and offer low-interest loans for health facilities, including hospitals and clinics.

Freeman said the president should propose funding significant programs in economic development but initially direct the secretary of agriculture to ask rural residents and community leaders for advice on investing resources to raise incomes and create jobs. This phase of the plan would be organized with citizen meetings across the United States to discuss reinventing the rural economy. Freeman would bring top officials of USDA agencies to the meetings, assigning each administrator and program director to meet with leaders from civic groups, local governments, and academic centers to discuss rural area development goals, policies, and programs. Eventually returning to their offices in Washington, D.C., with a clearer understanding of what rural communities needed and wanted, the officials could recommend to Secretary Freeman a set of economic development programs built from the ground up, programs that people in local communities would recognize had begun with local input following extensive consultation.

From the perspective of community leaders and local citizens in 1963, the prospect that federal officials would leave Washington, D.C., to come to local meetings was a radical concept. The idea that they would seek advice on raising incomes and creating jobs for a new mission was even more astonishing. But Freeman realized the federal teams, led by the secretary of agriculture and endorsed by the president, could generate enough political support for Congress to seriously consider new proposals by the Kennedy administration. The endorsement of the president was essential; otherwise the mission would be viewed as a Freeman initiative that could be ignored by those who could plead with Kennedy against the secretary.

The mission had several objectives, one of which was ending poverty in rural areas. Other objectives included a more diverse rural economy, better housing, safer water, an educational system to support a workforce with more diverse job skills, a health system that could serve the needs of a widely dispersed population, a flexible agriculture system as sensitive to nearby consumers as to global markets, and a credit system that did not tip the scales to impede access for small borrowers.

But the death of President Kennedy cut short the planning of Freeman's proposal.

Johnson, elected president in 1964 with the largest margin since Roosevelt, proposed the Office of Economic Opportunity (OEO) as a form of regional governance to end poverty by bringing economic opportunity to low income and economically disadvantaged individuals and groups. Since the greatest number of impoverished citizens lived in urban, inner-city areas, OEO focused resources on developing programs and projects in cooperation with bigger cities, effectively creating a hybrid of regionalism and cities while bypassing state government.

The War on Poverty generated enormous tensions at intergovernment and intragovernment levels. The conflict between the OEO (federal government) with state governments was obvious. The conflict between the USDA and the OEO arose not only because USDA's food policy and programs were Kennedy initiatives but also because food programs to eliminate hunger caused by poverty operated successfully through a state government network, while OEO evolved poverty program networks with big cities, bypassing state government.[2]

Another source of tension was the substantial level of federal funding allocated to OEO that other federal agencies resented because old-line agencies had other budget priorities. The funding conflict with USDA was unique because Freeman wanted to funnel more spending to food programs and to the mission of building a new rural economy.

If students of government had thought more deeply about what was evolving with Freeman's strategy on funding food programs, they might have realized it was a novel way of addressing the poverty issue. Hunger is caused by poverty that affects individuals not as solitary persons but as members of particular social groups.

Rural development activities in operation today largely continue the program structure organized by Secretary Freeman. Housing loans are available to rural residents without adequate housing who have incomes below 115 percent of the area's median income. The initial efforts to develop water systems and sewage treatment facilities have expanded to include a broad range of community facilities, including hospitals, fire protection, public safety, and other infrastructure services. As federal resources to create a new rural economy flowed, the USDA funded technical assistance and grant programs to support and improve community and economic development planning capabilities and to foster outreach and coordination of financial resources available from other than USDA sources.

The major reason Congress never tried to build a new rural economy may be contained in the data on appropriations for the USDA in the fiscal year (FY) 2010. The White House requested about $128 billion in overall spending, an amount Congress eventually agreed to authorize.

Food programs accounted for almost $90 billion, primarily to provide food stamps for 45 million people living in America and school meals for nearly 30 million school children.

Some $17 billion was allotted for farm income support, most of which was paid to fewer than 250,000 industrial farms. Rural development programs to strengthen rural community infrastructure, foster economic growth supporting job growth, and increase rural incomes for nearly 60 million Americans living in rural areas received about $17 billion, about the same as farm subsidies. The remaining $4 billion was allocated to other USDA programs, including food safety, research and data collection, forestry, and other services.

U.S. Secretary of Agriculture Freeman with agriculturists
in a field in India, 1964

8

The Prospect of Famine

Secretary of Agriculture Orville L. Freeman warned President Johnson in early November 1965 that India was months away from succumbing to a famine. The warning plunged the United States into a cascade of unexpected events over the next three years. These events, in both the United States and on the Indo-Pakistan subcontinent, lifted world hunger to one of the top global priorities for the next 20 years. They recast economic policy in India and dominated Johnson's interest in agriculture policy, unfortunately leading to decreased attention to economic reform in rural society in the United States.

The decision in the Oval Office that 20 to 30 million people in India should not be allowed to starve to death, an act of humanitarian impulse, was also a substantial policy commitment involving three policy sectors of the U.S. government. All three of them were committed to the singular goal of forestalling a famine, but the institutional objectives of each remained in conflict with those of the other.

One policy sector was agriculture, with institutional capacity in the USDA to foster agricultural production and food distribution, primarily on domestic programs. As a veteran of World War II, Secretary Freeman came to the USDA with a worldview aware of the importance of global conditions and the value of identifying economic, managerial, and research priorities (such as water and scientific research) related to food and agriculture. Both India and Pakistan were of special concern.

Another policy sector was the strategic interest of the United States—the institutional focus of the State Department and the national security apparatus within the White House. In 1965, while the war in Vietnam was heating up, the political stability of the Indo-Pakistan subcontinent was of high concern, but attention was focused on military conflict and the territorial ambitions of China.

The third policy sector was the institutional functioning of the office of the president. The political calculus of the institution required constant attention to Johnson's status as president so as to gauge his ability and capacity to set the policy objectives of the executive branch and to lead the country.

While all three sectors shared the goal of preventing famine, only Freeman could ensure it was achieved. Only the USDA had control of the grain reserves and the responsibility for managing a two-year supply of wheat in excess of domestic needs that the United States had stored as grain surplus. The USDA also had a staff with the management competence needed to transfer surplus wheat in the United States safely and in a timely manner to relieve the food deficit in India.

If Freeman could not manage the USDA to perform a humanitarian mission to save India, there would be no strategic issues in the Indo-Pakistan subcontinent to engage the State Department. The National Security Agency (NSA) staff members advising the president would have an entirely different set of issues to analyze. And if the

United States did not forestall an Indian famine in which 20 million people might starve to death, the political consequences for President Johnson could prove as devastating as the war in Vietnam eventually provided.

The effort to contain the impending famine and dispel its potent force could be neither ignored nor delayed while the United States expanded the war in Vietnam, fostered the civil rights movement, and engaged in the domestic War on Poverty. Turning back famine in the second most populous nation in the world could not be done overnight. It was a massive challenge, one that engaged the United States for three years in an intense managerial task of logistics and global politics second only to the demands of the war in Vietnam.

Those three years from 1965 through 1968—encompassing most of Johnson's term as president while inescapably entwining Freeman's tenure as secretary of agriculture in the history of the period—are examined over several chapters. Johnson inherited the war in Vietnam, but the imminent famine in India was an unexpected challenge.

The forces of famine had been gathering for years in India and on the Indo-Pakistan subcontinent since before India, the crown jewel in Great Britain's colonial empire, gained independence in 1947. The partition of India bequeathed by Britain upon its departure created Pakistan. The emergence of two nations in a bloody relationship on one subcontinent fostered war and military conflict as the means to resolve disputes over land, religion, economic advantage, and social dignity. The two nations shared a common land and widespread poverty where military expenditures consumed the scarce capital needed for investments.

The economies of both countries could support only a subsistence living for most citizens, nearly all of them living in rural areas and barely earning living. Most farmed with a technology largely unchanged for thousands of years. They survived precariously in a democracy but were ruled by Malthusian economics—that is, the population grew exponentially while food production was limited by the availability of land.

Faced with the option of spending limited cash for fertilizer or military hardware, both countries chose tanks and jet fighters over growing more food and investing in education and agricultural research. The United States and the Union of Soviet Socialist Republics (USSR or Soviet Union) provided military hardware as part of long-term sales agreements, but only the United States offered it in the massive quantities needed by India.

Both India and Pakistan, lacking international exchange to buy food, were locked in codependent relationships with the United States from the time of partition. The United States, overwhelmed by surplus grain threatening the economic survival of American farmers, could give its surplus grain to India and Pakistan. PL-480, authorized by Congress, provided for selling surplus grain and other agricultural commodities to impoverished countries on the condition that payment be isolated in accounts maintained by the United States in the recipient country. These funds could be used to finance social investment projects with the approval of the domestic government.

Neither India nor Pakistan had ever been able to feed its people. In 1965, the United States was shipping monthly about 500,000 tons of grain, mostly wheat, to India under the third five-year PL480 agreement with the United States. About one-fifth of that amount went to Pakistan. India, then with a population of about 500 million people, mostly Hindu, was the largest democracy in the world and the second most populous country (after China). Pakistan, with a population of 100 million, practiced Islam and had provided most of the recruited personnel for the British colonial military establishment. Indian leaders, frustrated by the United States seemingly paying as much attention to Pakistan with its 100 million people as to India with its 500 million, regularly complained that the American government couldn't count.

Jawaharlal Nehru, the lion of Indian politics who led the Congress Party in negotiating independence from Britain, had been India's prime minister since partition. By early 1965 the aged leader was dying. The constant pecking between India and Pakistan along their common border had drawn blood occasionally, but it escalated in August into a shooting war. Pakistan invaded disputed territory in Kashmir in northern India just as Nehru died. The Congress Party had to select his successor from the generation of new leaders who rose to power after independence. In the midst of India's struggle for new leadership and a shooting war in the Indo-Pakistan subcontinent, U Thant, secretary general of the United Nations from 1961 to 1971, called for the negotiation of a ceasefire agreement, with the United States and the Soviet Union working together quietly to build support for stopping the Kashmiri fire.

The Congress Party, with a vast majority in the India parliament, selected Lal Shastri, a respected leader, as prime minister. In September Shastri agreed to the ceasefire and to participate in negotiations to end the Kashmir conflict. USSR Premier Alexei Kosygin had offered to chair the negotiations, a proposition quietly backed by the United States. Gen. Ayub Khan, Pakistan's Prime Minister, rejected the UN offer of ceasefire negotiations, partly because the Pakistan forces had the momentum in the war. India had far larger combat forces, however, and eventually would overwhelm Pakistan's initial advantage. And the U.S. embassy in Rawalpindi passed along the view of President Johnson: "If Pakistan can spend some cash to pay for arms, then they can spend cash for the food they say they need. I don't see the United States [having] any obligation to send them 10 percent of the food they consume."

Shortly afterward, Gen. Ayub Khan agreed to participate with Shastri in the ceasefire negotiations in Tashkent, in the USSR in October. A ceasefire agreement was reached with the active participation of Premier Kosygin, and by early November arrangements were underway for Shastri to make a U.S. visit in early December to President Johnson. He never did; Shastri died suddenly in early November, just as another menacing development surfaced in India and the Indo-Pakistan subcontinent.

On November 11, R. W. Komer, special assistant to the president for national security, told McGeorge Bundy, Johnson's national security adviser, "We may have a major India food crisis on our hands." He also relayed that Freeman had sent a special observer to India to investigate reports of drought and crop failure. He was Lester Brown, an agricultural economist and foreign policy adviser with extensive knowledge of India. The news had already reached President Johnson, to whom Secretary Freeman had brought Brown's report from India that the country was poised on famine.

Secretary Freeman requested a meeting with President Johnson, not to deliver the news of an approaching famine but to present a plan to halt the famine before it could begin and a proposal to ensure that India would be able to feed itself in the future.

Freeman had convincing evidence to back his proposal, which would require the United States to ship a quarter of its annual wheat harvest to India. For one thing, the monsoons, an annual three-month deluge that fed rivers and streams, replenishing lakes and soil moisture, had failed to occur in India for two consecutive years. The special investigator he had dispatched to India three weeks earlier estimated parched fields would yield a grain crop in 1966 nearly a third below the normal harvest.

Further, India had exhausted its foreign exchange reserves in the war with Pakistan and was unable to pay cash for imports, leaving it dependent on monthly shipments of grain exports that were gifts from the United States. If realization that a famine was approaching spread through India, hoarding would begin. Access to existing food stocks would cease, sending the nation into a downward spiral of cascading food shortages, riots, and political chaos.

Freeman's thinking was the outgrowth of a two-week trip he took across India in early 1965 to study Indian agriculture. He had met at field level with local officials and educators to gain a hands-on understanding and later with government officials in New Delhi, India's capital, including Minister of Agriculture Chidanbaram (or C.) Subramaniam. The minister understood farm policy issues in India, and he knew the intractable policy conflict in the India cabinet between reformers and advocates of the Soviet model of industrial farming practices.

President Johnson listened as Freeman outlined his two-part plan. A quiet meeting could be arranged with Subramaniam to negotiate an agreement for the United States to ship more than a million tons of wheat monthly over the next year, twice the current U.S. food aid program for India. The second part of the agreement would be a reform package of Indian agricultural policies with the goal of raising Indian grain production. Freeman knew that the Indian cabinet and government agencies had blocked the changes Subramaniam wanted to bring to Indian agriculture policies and practices. They now could be incorporated as part of a historic mission to save the government and peoples of democratic India.

The meeting with Subramaniam could be arranged within the week in Rome, Freeman said, where ministers of agriculture were scheduled to meet November 19 for policy discussions at the headquarters of the United Nation's food and farm agency, the Food and Agriculture Organization (FAO). President Johnson had listened carefully to his secretary of agriculture. He gave approval to Freeman's plan—with several conditions.

Johnson was by nature a secretive politician who played the presidency game by holding his cards close to his chest. The U.S. embassy in Rome would know that Freeman and Subramaniam were conferring, Johnson said, but the objective of the meeting would not be revealed. Freeman could have one assistant from his own staff, but not a State Department officer, at the meeting. Freeman must not discuss the India project with anyone outside the secretary's office and the immediate program staff. He also must not discuss the project with the State Department or the Agency for International Development (AID).

Johnson especially did not want the U.S. embassy in New Delhi to know about the project until he was ready to reveal what would eventually be known as the Treaty of Rome (not to be confused with the 1957 founding document of European unification, which bears the same name). Johnson told the State Department only to arrange a meeting for Freeman with Subramaniam in Rome, ostensibly to discuss the agricultural situation in India.

President Johnson's decision to entrust to Secretary Freeman the mission to negotiate the Treaty of Rome, the U.S. program to shield India from famine in 1966–68, at first glance seems impulsive. The task should have been completed five years earlier by the U.S. State Department through its development bureau, AID. Complaining about the timing, however, begs the question of why Johnson agreed to Freeman's proposal to meet in Rome with Chidambaram Subramaniam to hammer out a solution to the failure of agriculture policy in India.

One possible reason is that presidents do not like surprises, do not like being caught unawares by untimely and unexpected events. Johnson probably lost confidence in the State Department and the U.S. embassy in New Delhi for failing to alert him to the approaching catastrophe revealed by his secretary of agriculture. But that is too simple a conclusion.

Famine is a cataclysmic tragedy, a crisis that does not occur suddenly or unexpectedly. It emerges from recognizable conditions that have been visible for years to both casual and knowledgeable observers. The U.S. embassy in New Delhi was one of those observers, its intelligence apparatus tasked to ensure that the American government was not surprised. U.S. policy was and is based on a careful evaluation of events and conditions and an awareness of situations. This requires strategic analysis and planning to ensure that the institutional interests of government agree on a course of action—it is a consensus process requiring time. This consensus was the responsibility of the National Security staff and may explain why foreign policy adviser McGeorge Bundy lectured Johnson on the need to handcuff Secretary Freeman's authority in Rome. Johnson dismissed the idea, and Freeman pointedly rejected it.

Freeman gave Johnson no reason to believe that the formal protocol of bureaucratic procedure of the State Department or the national security apparatus had failed as no consensus process had been initiated. Instead, Freeman came with a plan. The State Department had no plan, apparently because it was unaware of the crisis. Freeman would address the problem of famine as a crisis situation while equipping India with a change in long-term policy to raise agricultural productivity and improve the access of the people of India to a better diet.

The Treaty of Rome was not a departure from U.S. development policy. At a critical decision point, it was the first agreement with the Indian government to concisely incorporate AID recommendations. The agreement proposed to raise rice and wheat production in India by 25 percent in five years by creating a class of high-production farms operating on 32 million acres with access to virtually unlimited water and fertilizer resources. It authorized the Ministry of Food and Agriculture to override bureaucratic impediments by whatever means required. Domestic fertilizer production was to be subsidized and opened to unlimited investment by private companies from outside India.

The seeds for high-yield wheat and rice then coming to commercial availability, and later tagged the Green Revolution, were to be acquired regardless of initial cost. The agriculture credit market was to be flooded with cash, ending usury and driving credit costs to nearly zero. India's central government was to override state government policies that might impede the movement of production resources within India. The United States was to provide a five-year bridge of grain supplies over the period for implementing India's agricultural revolution to ensure adequate food supplies for the people.

That was the plan, and it worked. The treaty provisions required changes in policies and practices in every area of Indian agriculture policy, amounting to a revolution in Indian agriculture. Changes of this magnitude do not occur easily anywhere because agriculture is a set of practices and behavior that values tradition. That the research and development required to identify acceptable technologies had only recently rooted in India made it even harder.

An impending famine created the incentive to adopt revolutionary measures, opening the way for leadership that recognized the new policies and programs as revolutionary only in relation to realizing that maintaining the status quo was largely the cause of food shortages and famine. The willingness of the United Sates to open its bulging granary was the key element in the plan to reshape India's farm policy. It was an expression of U.S. confidence that the five-year plan would achieve its objective.

As president, Johnson needed to ensure that implementation of the two components of the plan would mesh seamlessly. This task required the hands-on direction of a person with intimate awareness and control of U.S. food and grain supplies, one also aware of the political complexities of ensuring access to food in India, a democracy twice as large at the United States, while initiating a revolution in farming practices in an agrarian society.

Johnson did not have time to rely on the institutional process of consensus building to produce a candidate. Within a matter of days, he had to find the person he could trust. Freeman had led the department through a major management reform, displayed astute political leadership in gaining congressional support for farm and food policy, impressed the political leadership in India, and negotiated an agreement the Indian government had approved—all in less than two weeks—and it was clearly endorsed by the policy apparatus of the U.S. government. Best of all, Johnson trusted Freeman's political instincts and his commitment to the president. Johnson could put Freeman in charge of implementing the Treaty of Rome as the natural choice.

Implicit in the Treaty of Rome was the moral obligation of the United States to accept responsibility for filling the gap between the food India could produce and the food its people needed to survive.

The five-year plan imbedded in the Treaty of Rome succeeded, confirming the judgment that supporting a revolution in agricultural policy in a democracy would benefit both the United States and India. Within three years grain production had recovered in India, and within five years India began to offer wheat for sale in global markets.

Secretary Freeman with Prime Minister Indira Gandhi,
New Delhi, India, ca. 1965

9

Confronting Famine and Saving Democracy

The Treaty of Rome was a brilliant global food policy strategy, a lesson plan for neutralizing famine, and a demonstration of famine as a political decision rather than a natural disaster. Weather may trigger the conditions essential to a famine, but so may failed agricultural policy. With the Treaty of Rome, the United States and India chose to stop a famine, thus emphasizing the importance of a system of trade to assemble and transport food grain, the availability of financial resources to pay financial costs, the authority to direct a complex but temporary project, and the ability to accurately measure food reserves—all openly and in public. There was only one great unknown: Was democracy in jeopardy?

Democracy was teetering on the brink of dismissal as a viable political system in South and Southeast Asia in 1966, not because of widespread popular global anger over the U.S. war in Vietnam, but because

India was descending into a famine. With a population of more than 500 million people at the time, India was the world's biggest functioning democracy. A famine there would destroy civil governance and social trust. Democracy could become the symbol of a failed political system unable to feed its people while the world's richest democracy, the United States, was capable only of waging war in Asia.

History records that India escaped the famine, and the official records establish that the motive for the U.S. policy to achieve this outcome was the humanitarian instinct President Johnson shared with Secretary Freeman, who initiated the rescue mission. Viewed from the results of Freeman's initiative, the ponderously deep political analysis of U.S. interests more commonly found in State Department cables and memos seem irrelevant today.

The official record of the Johnson administration for November/December 1965 and through 1968 is a trail of documents rich in intrigue and political infighting among federal agencies and power centers over the Treaty of Rome, negotiated to prevent famine and reform India's agriculture system. Failure to grasp the symbol of preserving democracy as an opportunity to reset U.S. policy objectives in an unwinnable war hangs with sad irony over all these events, as does the astonishing leadership of an American president who manipulated executive agencies as if they were elected senators.

Events as momentous as the decision by President Johnson to commit the equivalent of an estimated $2 billion in U.S. resources in 1966 to hold famine at bay in India are shrouded in confusion and confounded by conflicting memories. These facts are certain, however:

The United States held some 2 billion bushels of wheat in storage, twice the annual consumption rate of American consumers plus U.S. export sales and foreign-aid programs such as PL-480 (Food for Peace). The U.S. wheat stocks were, in fact, the world's global food reserve. That reserve joined India and the United States in a codependent relationship. From the end of World War II, the United States provided about 10 percent of India's annual food supply from surplus wheat production, which was growing faster than domestic consumption and exports combined. India had been skating on the edge of famine for nearly two decades, its condition masked by five-year agreements with the United States to fill its growing deficiency in food production. India was impoverished; it lacked the foreign-exchange reserves to purchase the food it needed because most Indians subsisted in an agricultural system that was failing.

Two billion bushels of wheat in storage posed an economic threat to farm prices in America's wheat belt. This provided a major incentive for the United States to negotiate the fourth in a series of PL-480 agreements with India late in 1965. These negotiations commanded the full attention of India's government and food industry as well as officials in the U.S. embassy on food assistance, blocking concern over an evident crop failure looming in the year ahead. The gap between Indian domestic production and food consumption had existed for more than 15 years and was always filled by food-aid agreements with the United States. Threat of a food shortage that would normally be signaled by rising food prices caused by a crop failure was dismissed by government officials and U.S. embassy staff in New Delhi as simply reflecting the delay in negotiating a new five-year agreement that would shortly be settled.

No similar consensus existed outside New Delhi, India's capital city. The monsoons, the annual deluge that ensured India's farmers enough water to grow the crops feeding themselves and India's people, had failed to develop for two consecutive years. Reservoirs were depleted, lakes were empty, streams were dry, and soil moisture had vanished. These conditions troubled the growing number of India's agricultural experts, a new profession that had emerged from India's heavy investment over the preceding 20 years in educational infrastructure with the help of the United States and the funding support of U.S. foundations. Scattered in rural areas, the experts saw the drought up close and had begun reaching out to contacts in the United States.

Some Indian experts contacted Secretary Freeman, whom they had met as he led a USDA team in 1963 visiting the agricultural education centers in India to assess progress and needs with Indian and U.S. experts. Now, as winter approached in the United States, Freeman heard a rising chorus from those individuals who were concerned that a crop failure in India might lead to widespread hunger regardless of conventional U.S. assistance programs.

Freeman discussed his concerns with other senior USDA officials, many of them involved in the PL-480 negotiations and equally worried about crop forecasts for India in 1966. Internal USDA memos, as well as press reports from India's newspapers, shared these elements: agreement that the conditions were a cause for concern but also that the situation could easily improve. And they avoided use of the word *famine*. In effect, everyone was waiting when time was the last resource to waste.

For an immediate assessment, the secretary sent a young economist recently returned from India and hired by the USDA: Lester Brown was to make a special survey of conditions in rural India. Halfway through a 10-day assessment trip in early November, Brown sent Freeman a cable confirming the worst suspicions of observers. Based on the assessments of experts, India's grain production would fall more than 10 million tons below levels of the previous year. U.S. grain shipments under PL-480 would normally provide 6 million tons a year, leaving a gap of 4 million tons. India was confronting a famine—it would need at least twice the assistance it had earlier.

In effect, U.S. policy toward India must be reshaped to include an emergency project to shield the country against famine while continuing the traditional assistance program for another five years. Freeman could take this recommendation to Secretary of State Dean Rusk, precipitating a bureaucratic free-for-all that would take several rounds of study and debate. Or he could go to the president.

The Rusk alternative would guarantee India's plunge into famine—Freeman was convinced that the window of opportunity to organize and carry out a massive rescue operation was rapidly closing. Going to President Johnson would involve days or several weeks, but it would place the burden of the decision to save India squarely on the president's shoulders. Why should Johnson believe Freeman? Freeman was not arguing geopolitics but rather a moral principle: the United States had the food, no other option was feasible, and very little time remained to make a decision.

In retrospect, Johnson's decision to follow the recommendations of his secretary of agriculture is understandable if not predictable. The awareness that president-elect Kennedy had winnowed his choice for vice president in 1960 to Johnson and Freeman was not far from President Johnson's mind. Kennedy believed Freeman was qualified to be president and to make the difficult choices that only the person who resides in the White House can make.

Johnson would have asked people he trusted to tell him openly of their views about Freeman. The president clearly based his decisions on conversations and discussions with other knowledgeable individuals. The memos he read were essentially those saying the time had come to decide. Among the first he would have spoken with was Charles Murphy, a Washington insider whom Johnson brought to the White House as a counselor from his post as undersecretary of agriculture under Freeman. Murphy had served as legal counselor to the Senate Agriculture Committee when Johnson was Senate majority leader. Before that position, Murphy had been an assistant to President Harry Truman in the White House from 1946 to 1950, when Johnson and Murphy had become acquainted.

Murphy admired Freeman for the wide respect he had gained within the USDA and for his leadership in organizing the USDA as an agency capable of developing and managing public programs and service. If Freeman said the USDA could take on a project, Murphy knew the project would be done and on schedule. Murphy was impressed with Freeman's ability to work with legislative leaders in both the House and the Senate, a political skill not displayed by most agriculture secretaries.

Johnson would also have asked veteran senators of the South, who ruled the upper chamber, such as Allen Ellender, alumnus of Louisiana politics and chair of the Senate Agriculture Committee. Johnson knew these men well—he once complained that Freeman could cajole them to do things for the secretary of agriculture they would not do for the president.

Freeman wanted to meet with C. Subramaniam, India's minister of food and agriculture, to negotiate an agreement that would provide India with enough grain to avoid a famine and a package of policy and program reforms to increase India's agricultural productivity. The reforms were a set of organizational and procedural steps widely supported in India among economists and scientists within the emerging agricultural educational system. But their passage had been stymied in India's cabinet by ministers whose ideological views on farm policy slowed acceptance of scientific and technological advance.

Subramaniam, whom U.S. Ambassador to India Chester Bowles considered a good friend of the United States, was an advocate of agricultural reform. Freeman proposed that the two agricultural politician leaders meet in Rome, where agricultural ministers and secretaries of the world were gathering shortly for a conference at the Food and Agricultural Organization (FAO), the UN agricultural agency. Discussion among government representatives was a normal part of those events, and Freeman and Subramaniam's meeting would attract little or no attention.

Johnson approved the Rome meeting but wanted Freeman and Subramaniam to understand that any draft agreement had to be approved by the president. Johnson was giving Freeman a free hand to draft a plan, but he instructed Freeman to divulge the extent of his authority to no one. An assistant but no one else—no one from the U.S. embassy in Rome and no one from Subramaniam's staff—could accompany him in the negotiations. Johnson was to tell his White House foreign policy staff and Secretary Rusk that Freeman would meet in Rome with Subramaniam to discuss India's food and agriculture situation and that Freeman would be accompanied by only one person from his USDA staff. Johnson gave Freeman no written instructions; he told the White House staff and the State Department that he had asked Freeman to meet with Subramaniam and report back to the president. When foreign policy adviser McGeorge Bundy learned of it later, all hell broke loose.

Bundy clearly considered Freeman an interloper, an outsider who did not participate in foreign policy affairs and who had no authority to negotiate agreements with other countries. He moved quickly to repair what he considered a breach of his own authority in the White House power structure. He called Freeman to a meeting, the results of which Bundy reported in a November 17 memo to the president, the last one he wrote to Johnson about India and farm and food policy.

In his memo, Bundy insisted that Freeman bring Subramaniam back to Washington when he returned from Rome, which would have put the Indian minister in the firm hands of Bundy and the State Department. Bundy acknowledged Freeman's rejection of this option by pointing out that if Subramaniam left Rome empty-handed he couldn't be seen to beg in Washington for what he could not get in Rome.

Freeman and Bundy agreed that the president's freedom to make the final decision could not be compromised. Bundy also agreed that Freeman must be able to negotiate with Subramaniam but only on condition that the secretary of state and the secretary of the treasury, along with the heads of AID and the Office of Management and Budget (OMB), sign off on any outcome of the discussions. In effect, Bundy told President Johnson that he could make a final decision only on the portion of any proposed agreement not vetoed by his own appointees. The memo warned Freeman that Bundy would tie up indefinitely any proposal emerging from his discussions with Subramaniam.

Bundy's memo also suggested that a split on India policy existed in his own national security staff. Bundy, the State Department, and Ambassador Bowles believed Subramaniam's key objective was a U.S. loan to purchase fertilizer to raise crop yields. Bundy's deputy, Robert W. Komer, disagreed, indicating that the prospects for a poor harvest in 1965 made food aid the most important outcome of the Rome discussions. Although Komer had no previous knowledge of Johnson authorizing Freeman to negotiate an agreement, Komer recognized immediately that Freeman would return from Rome with a proposed agreement the president would likely accept.

Komer had first raised this view in a November 16 memo to President Johnson discussing the status of United States-India relations. Aware of Johnson's dislike of long memos, Komer advised: "If you don't want to read this memo, scan these points." Komer neatly summarized the current status of relations as basic satisfaction with India's policies but concern over India's performance. He suggested that no change in U.S. policy was needed, "so the United States should bargain massive aid for sharply improved performance, especially in agriculture."

"The sooner we can strike the bargain, the better for the United States," Komer informed the president, unaware of Freeman's intent in the negotiations with Subramaniam that would begin in three days, on November 19. Komer clearly anticipated the historical outcome on November 25 of what would become known as "The Treaty of Rome."

In Rome, Freeman and Subramaniam agreed to a cable written together that the secretary sent for the president's eyes only, summarizing the dire food shortage facing India in 1966 and explaining the basis for the massive food-aid package to come:

Earlier estimates of grain production optimistic. 1964–65 crop production of 88 million ton will drop by 10 million to 78 million ton. Drought most serious of this century. Virtually every area of India hit. Current actual consumption estimated at 174 kg per capita well below minimum FAO standard. If 10 million ton less available, intake to drop to 152 kg per capita. Prediction that 10 million cut in food grain would result in substantial starvation is valid.

The cable, widely circulated in the U.S. government and American embassies, was a strike of lightning, illuminating in a split second the changed nature of the challenge to U.S. foreign policy and the threat to the government of India. The scramble was on to develop new strategy in Washington and New Delhi, but Johnson was already reading the proposal by Freeman and Subramaniam as to how both governments should proceed.

The Treaty of Rome was a plan of action reflecting Freeman's organizational mind, one detailing a pledge of massive U.S. assistance and the commitment of India to a wide-ranging reform project that would remake its agricultural practices.[1] John P. Lewis, director of the U.S. AID program in India, described the agreement as "more solid in content and promise than any comparable program since [India's] Independence." Lewis said the United States "has helped engineer what could be a breakthrough for the Indian agricultural expansion." The World Bank viewed the agreement as a major part of a "Big Push" to speed up economic growth in India.

At this early stage, the nature of the task ahead for the United States and India was not fully understood. The picture became clearer in Komer's December 6 memo to the president stating that conventional monthly shipments of 500,000 tons of grain were no longer a credible response to India's food needs. The shortfall in grain, estimated at 10 million tons in 1966, had been revised to 20 million tons. Komer wrote: "The sheer magnitude of India's food crisis" required the United States "to go big to be generously responsive."

Komer noted that the United States and India faced daunting logistical challenges, including India's limited port capacity. India had never recorded annual grain imports of more than 7 million tons from oceangoing carriers, well below the level of grain supply India needed. In addition to logistical issues, public perception was a potential problem, Komer warned. Widespread hoarding in India could reduce food supplies further. Only the general belief that the United States was aware of the threat of a food shortage and prepared to send assistance on a massive scale had held it in check. Statements raising doubts about whether the United States would "go big" must be avoided.

The response of India's government was also a significant factor. Subramaniam returned from Rome in early December to begin organizing the massive distribution of food assistance, but first he needed to obtain the commitment of the Indian government to the agricultural reforms outlined in the Treaty of Rome. Freeman prodded Subramaniam in a December 2 cable to Ambassador Bowles approved by President Johnson. The secretary asked Bowles to inform Subramaniam that Freeman had reviewed the Rome agreement with President Johnson, "who is pleased with the steps taken and contemplated by the Indian government to improve Indian agriculture." The secretary informed Subramaniam that Johnson was looking forward to Subramaniam's discussion with the India cabinet outlining the points agreed to in Rome. He noted that Johnson was actively considering the amount and period of the PL-480 extension as well as the fertilizer loan request.

In effect, Freeman was telling Subramaniam—and the U.S. State Department and U.S. embassy, as well as the government of India— that pending the acceptance of the India government, Johnson was prepared to carry out the U.S. commitments of the Treaty of Rome. The ball was in Subramaniam's court, and he acted quickly.

Over the next week Subramaniam met with the Council of State, India's cabinet, proposing a historic reform of agricultural policy in India that would incorporate his commitment to change Indian farm policy first outlined in the Treaty of Rome. After two days of intense and often angry debate, the council agreed to Subramaniam's reforms, essentially putting him in charge of agricultural development and the food distribution program that would save India from famine.

Johnson signaled his favorable response on December 9, announcing a three-month 1.5 million-ton expansion of U.S. grain exports under the PL-480 agreement and a $50 million loan for the purchase of fertilizer. The fertilizer, according to agricultural experts, was equivalent to 4 million tons of additional grain production.

A week later the president said the U.S. commitment to assist India was unconditional and unlimited. He directed Freeman to create a special committee within the U.S. government to use "all available resources you deem necessary to cope with the looming Indian famine." The committee was to include the secretaries of state, defense, and commerce, the administrator of AID, and other agencies Freeman wanted. In a National Security Action Memorandum (No. 339), Johnson directed Secretary Freeman to "recommend whatever imaginative technique and device which may be necessary," effectively authorizing Freeman to run the rescue mission. The president, emphasizing that he was "deeply concerned on humanitarian grounds," used the word *famine* for the first time in official documents to describe the nature of the crisis.

Less than a month had passed since Freeman and Subramaniam sat together in a conference room in the U.S. embassy in Rome with Lester Brown. In three days they had written a plan that would work, that would awaken the world to a pending famine that no one had publicly recognized. It changed government policy in India and the United States in two weeks and transformed a proposal into the Treaty of Rome in 10 days. The original drafting partners were in charge of saving millions of people from starvation and restoring the uncertain future of democracy.

The heaviest lifting was yet to come.

A plan is a political document meant to minimize opposition and assign organizational control. The problem in a famine is logistics: how to move a vast amount of food in an incredibly short time within the traditional internal distribution channels—before the destructive economic and social forces unleashed in a famine render the plan useless.

Both Freeman and Subramaniam were effective managers and superb organizers. Subramaniam was the inside man responsible for deploying one-third of U.S. wheat stocks, or the global wheat reserve, through India in one year. Freeman was the outside man responsible for organizing the stationing of 15 million tons of wheat at U.S. ports, of scheduling a fleet of oceangoing grain vessels to carry the grain across the Pacific Ocean and deliver it to Indian ports for timely internal transfer to Indian markets.

Movement of the grain was the key element in the mammoth enterprise. Freeman was confident that the Foreign Agriculture Service, the USDA agency responsible for scheduling the shipments of U.S. grain under PL-480 contracts, could handle contracting the India grain shipments. The United States, however, relied on the operations of U.S. grain exchanges to contract the positioning of grain supplies. And it relied on the U.S. grain trade to initially finance and coordinate the rail and barge movement of grain as well to contract the ships ensuring timely delivery to India's ports.

A good manager never goes into a major project without contingency preparations. Even with maximum effort, India's port facilities could not handle more than 7 million tons of grain shipments a year without a major expansion of facilities, and construction would take years. The USDA leased a huge grain carrier as a temporary facility, anchoring the vessel off the harbor of Bombay. The ship was outfitted to offload grain onto smaller vessels that could get into smaller port facilities on the Indian subcontinent and deliver smaller quantities of grain that the Indian government could schedule for delivery by rail to interior markets. Grain shipments from the United States replenished the grain supply in the offloading ship anchored near Bombay. The arrangement was a key part of the project.

In case Subramaniam's logistics schedule should become overwhelmed internally and threaten to create brief but potentially calamitous food shortages in some regions of India, Freeman had a backup plan. He arranged with Secretary of Defense Robert McNamara, his avid opponent in weekly handball games, to organize emergency food-distribution operations using U.S. helicopters and other air cargo carriers to deliver grain and other emergency food stocks. The backup plan was never needed or unleashed.

A significant element of the Treaty of Rome was the plan to catapult domestic wheat production in India by introducing new varieties that otherwise would not have reached India's farmers as seed for several years. The United States lent funds to India to purchase all the wheat available from Mexico for export in 1965–66, not as a food source but as seed for India's next harvest.

Mexican farmers had just harvested the first commercial planting of a new short-stemmed wheat variety developed at the International Maize and Wheat Improvement Center in Mexico. The short-stemmed variety was the first major crop of a vanguard of higher-yield varieties of grain in the vaunted green revolution sweeping the world in the 1960s. Indian researchers already had tested the new variety in the Punjab, India's wheat belt, with outstanding results, but India lacked the international exchange to pay cash for Mexico's exports. The short-stemmed wheat variety, while consuming more water than conventional varieties, put more energy into producing grain than in growing the plant's stem, especially with chemical fertilizer and abundant water supplies.[2]

Combined with the provisions to expand fertilizer production in India and open the India market to commercial fertilizer imports, the widespread adoption of the short-stemmed wheat variety led to record wheat harvests in India with the return of the monsoons after 1966. The turnaround was remarkable. Within five years India began commercial exports of wheat, transforming the crop into building rather than consuming international exchange earnings.

Freeman's initiative to confront the emergence of famine as a social and economic tragedy required the meshing of political and commercial components within a narrow time frame in which delay could be fatal, as famine is a descent into social chaos that cannot be halted.

One component of the successful initiative was its clarity of authority. At the outset, McGeorge Bundy, as foreign policy adviser, had challenged Freeman while the State Department and the U.S. embassy in India sat on the sidelines. All the centers of political power, including the government of India, had the information available to Freeman, but they seemed incapable of grasping its meaning or acting on its implications. The first use of the word *famine* in describing the crisis appeared in President Johnson's National Security Action memo of December 17, putting Freeman in charge of enactment of the Treaty of Rome—the plan to confront the crisis that Freeman and Subramaniam had written nearly a month earlier.

Another component was a definable food reserve, in this case the two-year domestic supply of U.S. wheat in storage, isolated from commercial markets as the world's food reserve. In addition to U.S. wheat surpluses, the commercial pipeline of wheat, rice, and other food grains in the United States, globally essential to market stability, was to be included in global food reserves in a way left intentionally vague so as to thwart speculators and market manipulators seeking profit in volatile commodity prices and uncertain markets.

Another component was the commercial grain trade, operating through commodity exchanges where grain was bought and sold and where commercial traders purchased and sold contracts to deliver grain in international trade, moving grain and food commodities from surplus to deficit regions and countries. International trade in grain essentially is trade in grain surpluses. The U.S. government sold wheat from surpluses held in storage to supply the wheat needed in India, ensuring stable grain prices in the United States and protecting American consumers from higher prices. Grain traders bought wheat on U.S. commodity exchanges, contracted with shipping companies to deliver the wheat to India ports, and managed the transfer of U.S. wheat to India. Commodity exchanges and trading companies were indispensable to implementing the Treaty of Rome.

Another essential component was funding. India alone lacked the financial resources to carry the project to completion, and the United States funded the implementation of the agreement. Although no estimate of the overall cost emerged formally, the cost of completing the Treaty of Rome likely exceeded $2 billion. The USDA had already paid for the grain it purchased from U.S. growers and was storing at government expense. One of the unique benefits of federal accounting was that the project could be shown on the books as producing substantial savings in storage costs and losses from wheat spoilage. But someone or some entity had to pay the "overhead" costs—the expense incurred in handling the gathering and movement of the grain from U.S. storage across the Pacific Ocean to India.

Identifying the elements of managing a plan to confront famine begs the ultimate question, however. How do nations recognize a crisis is building and avoid a waste of time in negotiations confronting the crisis? No mechanism for a "famine watch," which might have brought the United States or others to the conclusion reached by Freeman, existed in 1965. Furthermore, no relationship such as that of the confidence between Freeman and President Johnson—essential to making decisions within a limited time—is easily replicated. Yet these elements are necessary in a world continuing an uneasy drift into an era in which maintaining large food reserves is no longer possible.

Secretary Freeman consulting with Indian farmers, ca. 1965

10

The Political Challenge of Preempting Famine

A protocol for defending against famine did not exist in 1965. Neither did copies of protocols for defending against the Irish famine in the 19th century or any of the historic famines that swept various parts of the world.[1] The reason is obvious. The word describes a tragedy, a famine, as a historical event.

No plan of action had been made to deal with the consequences of a protracted shortage of food in which civil society ceased to function. No famine was described in pre-biblical Egypt, for example, when Joseph's brothers fled the famine foresight for seven years while the Nile fully flowed. Then the seven years of drought engulfed the region, leading Joseph's brothers to their family reunion in Egypt.

Without becoming enmeshed in biblical history or the exegesis of grain stores, Secretary Freeman and Minister Subramaniam wrote a protocol in 1965 to preempt a famine. They wrote an agreement in three days to work together to prevent millions of people living on the Indian subcontinent from starving to death. They wrote the protocol in full over the three years they guided both governments and the private sector in containing as they reacted daily to unfolding events.

The India famine of 1965–1968 differed from its predecessors in several respects. Preemption proved a successful strategy. A definite date can be established for the famine's beginning and end. In previous famine events, those who survived as participants or witnesses estimated the beginning of the historic calamity. The India famine began when President Johnson used the word *famine* on December 12, 1965, in a statement pledging U.S. grain stores to shield India from the calamity. The famine ended in April 1968, when Secretary Freeman met with India's ambassador to the United States to discuss the commercial purchase of U.S. wheat in response to India's notice of intent to purchase wheat for cash on global markets. The end of the famine occurred when India subsequently offered wheat for sale on global markets in 1970.

The decision to confront an approaching famine changes the definition of the event. Before President Johnson's announcement, famine was considered the act of an angry God or the consequence of natural events, mainly weather, one synonymous with the other. However the cause was perceived, the disaster was assumed beyond human control. After 1965, famine was defined as a political outcome, a human condition that people and nations may choose to preempt as an issue of public policy—or allow to occur out of moral cowardice.

The appropriate definition was still in question in December 1965, when Secretary Freeman and Minister Subramaniam began implementing the Treaty of Rome. As they found success, the definition of *famine* as a political event emerged in 1968 as India's agriculture was restored. And through their acceptance of the responsibility to cooperate internationally to contain famine, a policy framework for the international human right to food emerged as a global mission (as yet unfulfilled).

Nothing so high-flown was part of Subramaniam and Freeman's agenda when they returned to their home nations from Rome in 1965. Wheat and other food grains were stored in the hundreds of towering grain elevators of the American plains—thousands of miles from the hungry people. Logistics—the creation and management of a food pipeline—was an overwhelming challenge. Within weeks, millions of tons of grain had to begin moving from storage along the Missouri and the Mississippi Rivers on carefully planned schedules by barge, train carrier, and truck into oceangoing ships in ports on the Gulf of Mexico (mainly New Orleans) and the U.S. West Coast. While Freeman primarily confronted the logistics, Subramaniam not only had the task of planning the timing and movement of food within India as it was unloaded at seaports but also that of confronting the issues of reform—removing the political inertia encrusting India's domestic policies, which had caused the crisis.

The timing of grain shipments was crucial to success. The scheduling of grain shipments from U.S. elevators had to be geared to the availability of ship bottoms at U.S. ports to avoid a supply buildup that would clog ports while providing a backup for the movement of domestic grain. At the same time, grain carriers must be moving regularly on the Gulf of Mexico and across the Pacific, their arrival timed to match the unloading capability of Indian ports.

The maximum annual capacity of Indian ports to handle grain imports was 7 million tons, or slightly less than 600,000 tons monthly. Freeman and Subramaniam agreed India would need average monthly shipments of about a million tons during all of 1966 and probably 1967—60 percent more than it had the physical capacity to handle.

They resolved the dilemma with an ingenious plan. They would lease an oceangoing tanker for anchorage in the port of Bombay, modified to offload grain directly into small cargo carriers that could easily access the smaller ports dotting India's coastline. The tanker had a maximum capacity of 200,000 tons of grain and could offload 5,000 to 10,000 tons of grain monthly to each of several dozen smaller cargo ships. The tanker provided a useful supplement to India's movement of grain from seaports into the country's interior by allowing wider dispersion of wheat and other food grains more rapidly than would be possible by rail alone.

The keystone of success for the U.S. phase of the Treaty of Rome was the managerial skill of the international grain trade, a commercial enterprise of European and U.S. companies dominating the movement of agricultural commodities in modern times from regions of surplus to populations where deficits exist. Grain traders have honed their competence since before history was written. Even the cuneiform tablets of ancient Babylon summarize the daily practices of commodity traders. Egypt was Rome's breadbasket, courtesy of the grain trade, and the mini-famines that plagued medieval Italy ended when the Hanseatic League traders on the Baltic Sea found that the Russian czars had surplus wheat that could be bought cheaply and sold dearly in Italy.

Trading companies would keep the pipeline functioning in 1966—they had 14 years of experience in ensuring that the smaller volumes of PL-480 grain from the United States arrived in India in timely manner. The immediate task for Freeman was to plan a strategy to manage the U.S. logistics operation and coordinate timing issues with a counterpart operation in India linked to the U.S. embassy staff. The task of managing the pipeline of grain was assigned to the Agriculture Stabilization and Conservation Service (ASCS), the USDA agency that managed the billion-dollar Commodity Credit Corporation (CCC).[2] ASCS would finance the rescue of India. The mission of ASCS was to manage farm surpluses that formed the bulk of U.S. food reserves, promote stable markets for consumers, and improve farm income. ASCS owned or held loans in 1965 on billions of dollars of farm and food commodities and had the authority and dollars to spend whatever was necessary.

The cost of the grain that ASCS already owned did not involve new government spending—it was technically a matter of bookkeeping. The agency's staff, along with staff from USDA's Foreign Agriculture Service (FAS), contracted for what became a fleet of nearly 600 ships, placed orders for the grain to fill the ship bottoms, and paid all the bills until ownership of the grain was transferred as a PL-480 sale to the Indian government.

Freeman had two other contentious tasks. One was to brief Congress on the Treaty of Rome while keeping the agriculture committees of the House and Senate informed of the status of the project. The other was to keep pace with President Johnson's burgeoning awareness and interest in the unexplored potential of food as power in the ballet of international policy. While many domestic issues confronting the department—particularly rural development—might have benefited from Johnson's attention, he directed his interest with laser intensity to the Indian famine and U.S. strategy on the India subcontinent.

Freeman's immediate concern was Congress. Had Congress been asked in December 1965 to register its concern about a potential threat of famine in India, the answer on a scale of one to ten likely would have been somewhere below zero. The general public was unaware of any problem, and no senator or representative had raised the issue as a matter of legislative interest. Johnson recognized the political peril of moving quickly to preempt the famine ahead of public opinion. He wanted to anticipate any political opposition before it could be organized.

Secretary Freeman was in a strong position to respond to congressional unease. He had developed an effective working relationship with the House and Senate in gaining approval for a new farm program that had general support. And the new food policies represented by the Food Stamp program and reforms in child nutrition programs were beginning to take hold. Freeman's four missions to access conditions in India over the previous two years enabled him to speak from an eyewitness perspective. The farm-state legislators mindful of urban congressional criticism of costly surplus grain storage could note with pride that farm policies made the India initiative possible and that the project would put to beneficial use food resources larger than United States needed for reserves.

Secretary of State Dean Rusk and Secretary Freeman jointly testified in December before the Senate Agriculture Committee on the new U.S. commitment to contain a famine and support far-reaching reforms in India's agricultural economy. Freeman described the background leading up to his meeting in Rome with Minister Subramaniam, explaining the key features of the Treaty of Rome. He also reviewed the status of U.S. wheat reserves and discussed the plans under development to move record levels of wheat to India. Rusk provided an assessment of the situation in India from the perspective of the U.S. embassy, explaining why conditions had worsened decisively in recent days, and said that all U.S. agencies were coordinating efforts at the direction of President Johnson to forestall a famine in India. That Johnson had been reelected by the largest electoral college margin in history clinched the proposal to preempt the India famine.

The impact of the hearing and of personal visits by Freeman and Rusk with congressional leaders reassured Congress that the United States had recognized a threat to the stability of the Indian subcontinent and was taking decisive action at a time when the United States was involved in a deteriorating military action elsewhere in Southeast Asia.[3] In effect, the danger was in hand, and the United States was in control. Johnson was satisfied the political fences had been tested and found to be strong and safe.

The congressional hearing neither raised nor addressed the long-term implications of containing a famine in India. But the implications were beginning to form in President Johnson's thoughts. For one thing, Lyndon Johnson wanted to know in early February 1966 what India was going to do for him, casting the personal pronoun as a reference for the United States. On February 2 he discussed at some length with Secretary Freeman what he wanted to say in a meeting he would hold shortly with B. T. Nehru, India's ambassador to the United States. Summary notes of Johnson's conversation with Freeman are pithy and colloquial, revealing as much about Johnson's relations with his advisers as of his policy views. He did not ask Freeman for advice but instead used the occasion as a sounding board to instruct the secretary of agriculture in shaping his handling of the Indian rescue mission.

"I'm waiting to see what kind of foreign policy we can have with your people," Johnson said in outlining the message the president wanted Nehru to convey to India's leaders. "It's not going to be a one-way deal. I'm not going to just underwrite the perpetuation of the government of India and the people of India to have them spend their time dedicating themselves to the destruction of the people of the United States and the U.S. government."

President Johnson continued, "We're going to just sit here until they find it in their interest to come and discuss and negotiate, to outline what it is they want us to do. If all they want is for me to deliver some money to them, then I'm not going to be interested. I'm interested in them helping us, too. How can they help us? What can they do to help us?

"I'm by implication committed to giving India 10 million tons of wheat. I get 14 memos from State, Agriculture, Komer, Bundy, and so on as to what to do. I don't want to do it that way," Johnson said. "When I put my wheat down, and it costs us several hundred million, I want to see what you're putting on the other side. And, if it's just a bunch of bullshit and a lot of criticism of the president, that's a different thing."

And what did President Johnson want?

"I would think they could help us if they understood our objectives and our viewpoint and try to be sympathetic. I don't just say rubberstamp everything we do, but they don't need to denounce us every day on what we're doing in Vietnam," Johnson said, summarizing for Freeman what he intended to say to Ambassador Nehru.

Two days after meeting with Nehru, President Johnson announced an additional PL-480 agreement to send to India 3.5 million tons of wheat plus a million tons of milo, which was used there as food for humans as well as for animals. He followed this action to ensure a full pipeline of U.S. grain with a special message to Congress on February 10 in which he proposed a new "Food for Freedom" policy.

Johnson said the United States was concerned about the rising levels of world hunger, citing the approaching famine in India. He described the actions being taken by the United States in the Treaty of Rome with India and outlined the plan to mobilize U.S. grain reserves to preempt the India famine. In addition, he said the United States was asking nations around the world to join in support of the India government efforts to protect its citizens from hunger and starvation.

Secretary Rusk subsequently reported that 113 nations had been contacted, 35 of which provided the equivalent of $150 million in cash and commodities to assist India. In a summary report to President Johnson, Special Assistant for National Security Affairs Walt Rostow noted that the most striking aspect of the nations contacted was how many were on the emergency list of those considered most vulnerable to food shortages. Congress approved a join resolution April 19 to "support U.S. participation in relieving victims of hunger in India and to enhance the capacity of India to meet the nutritional needs of its people." On November 11, 1966, within a year of the Treaty of Rome agreement with India, it adopted the "Food for Peace Act."

Imperceptibly but with remarkable speed, U.S. national security policy was shifting to encompass global food priorities. The transition was evident in July 19 comments by President Johnson in chairing the National Security Council. He said, "Hunger is a national security mission with a focus on world food problems. The size and urgency of the problem requires a worldwide attack on hunger," noting that the U.S. public resists routine assistance to foreign countries.

Secretary Rusk said the "fight on hunger must include nations other than food-producing countries," implying that the U.S. strategy relied on raising food production in all countries, not just the nations exporting food. AID administrator David Bell supported his view, saying, "Agriculture programs must be integrated in the national economy of all developing nations."

Briefing the meeting, Secretary Freeman summarized the effort underway to preempt famine in India, describing the status of programs to provide seed, ensure water availability, and secure access to fertilizer.

"India is on track to become self-sufficient in food," he said. "The government of India is living up to its commitments, and now the United States needs to do the same."

Vice President Hubert H. Humphrey said the United States needed to increase wheat production to ensure an adequate carryover of wheat stocks to block speculation in commodity prices and minimize inflation and rising food prices.

Later that month, Freeman reviewed the status of the U.S. intervention in India's food situation with President Johnson, noting that the estimate made in December 1965 of an 18-million-ton shortfall in grain production was accurate. He said Subramaniam had asked the United States for 11 to 12 tons of grain in food assistance and reported that grain was arriving monthly in India at the rate of about a million tons: "Currently, U.S. shipments will reach about 8 million tons for the year. Another 1.5 million tons will be provided in the combined form of assistance from other nations and in equivalent increases in fertilizer imports."

Freeman said the United States must make an additional commitment of about 1.8 million tons of grain in 1966, bringing the overall level of food assistance for the year to more than 11 million tons of grain. He described the U.S. commitment as "one of the greatest movements globally of food in all time."

Early reports of the U.S. wheat harvest in 1966 suggested expectation of a 6 percent drop in production, surprising news that, combined with the volume of grain shipments to India, led to speculation pushing up wheat prices in the grain futures market. Adding to the speculation was the news that U.S. wheat stocks in storage had dropped from a record 40 million to about 30 million, still a level nearly twice the U.S. wheat reserve requirement for stable food prices.

By late August President Johnson was concerned. He was uneasy about the rising bread prices blamed by baking companies on higher wheat prices caused by market speculation. He asked economists in the Office of Management and Budget to study whether the shipments of grain to India could be blamed for speculation in wheat prices. OMB reported in early September that the U.S. response to famine in India had no measurable influence on wheat prices and that its effect on bread prices was negligible.

Official production reports in September estimated that the U.S. wheat output in 1966 was nearly 2 million tons more than in1965, deflating speculative pressures in commodity futures markets as buffer U.S. wheat stocks strengthened. Abundant wheat harvests in the northern hemisphere immediately generated demands from growers that the government do more to strengthen wheat prices.

The drop in grain prices as speculation waned had the unintended effect of increasing PL-480 shipments to India. The USDA team managing the grain pipeline reported in October that an additional 250,000 tons, more than a million bushels of wheat, was released for shipment to India. With lower market prices, the tonnage could be increased within the limits of authorized funding. The program could make both U.S. farmers and the Indian people happier, without upsetting U.S. consumers.

As the first anniversary of the Treaty of Rome approached, a broader and more exhaustive assessment of the strategy to preempt the India famine began. The summer's optimism about efforts to prevent starvation did not extend to the longer-term reforms in agriculture policy outlined in the Treaty of Rome to strengthen India's agriculture and food production.

Secretary Freeman gave the news to President Johnson with Secretary of State Dean Rusk and Special Assistant for National Security Affairs Walt Rostow concurring.

"The monsoons failed to appear in 1966. India's grain harvest, initially estimated at 85 million tons of wheat—or 10 million tons lower than normal—was about 79 million tons. India continued to lag in fertilizer imports and production, pesticide distribution, and seed distribution," Freeman reported. "Subramaniam is committed to the Treaty of Rome, but the government of India is committed to business as usual, negotiating for fertilizer imports by bargaining for advantage on price. The government is using the agency created to support farm prices to instead procure grain at below market prices. The effect is to drive down farm income, cutting food production."

Freeman concluded that Prime Minister Indira Gandhi was not committed to the Treaty of Rome. He recommended that Johnson "keep Gandhi on a short leash" with the minimum PL-480 allocations needed to keep the grain pipeline functioning. The United States should not expect major changes in government policy until after Indian national elections in February and appointment of a new government.

The Treaty of Rome had forestalled a famine in India, Freeman told Johnson, but the threat remained for 1967. He recommended, with the concurrence of Rusk and Rostow, that Johnson approve an interim agreement for 2 million tons of wheat, with review of the situation in December.

Ambassador Bowles denounced Freeman's memo as "extraordinarily insensitive."

President Johnson excoriated the secretary in a telephone call for an entirely different reason: "You gave the best damned argument I ever saw for not giving aid to India. You said they hadn't kept their agreement on fertilizer and outside investment and hadn't had the follow-though necessary to keep the agreement, that India is discouraging food production rather than stimulating it."

"I can't take a recommendation like yours and feed India for another year. We're giving them a billion dollars, and our grain surpluses are being depleted," Johnson fumed, recognizing that Freeman had identified the central political problem in building support for a new policy on the War of Hunger.

The president asked Freeman to send a team of experts to India to find out whether India had met its Treaty of Rome commitments and to evaluate the conditions going into 1967 through examination of changes underway in the government there. At the same time, he asked Congress to appoint a special delegation of senators and representatives to make an onsite assessment of food and agriculture conditions in India and to report back its findings and recommendations by the end of the year.

Ambassador Bowles was livid, complaining in a long cable to Secretary Rusk that sending a USDA team to assess India's performance under the Treaty of Rome was a slap in the embassy's face, suggesting the president had no confidence in the ability of the embassy to give a balanced assessment. He refused to deliver a letter from Freeman to Subramaniam asking him to assist the team; instead he conveyed the request verbally.

Subramaniam told Bowles he welcomed the USDA team and the forthcoming visit of the congressional delegation as he did "any effort that will create better understanding of India's needs."

The USDA team concluded that the government of India achieved in the first year of the treaty about 80 percent of what it had agreed to do. Congress agreed to establish a special delegation—led jointly by Texas Democrat William R. Poage, chair of the House Agriculture Committee from 1967 to 1975, and Kansas Republican Dole, ranking minority member of the Senate Agriculture Committee—to make recommendations to President Johnson on India.

Secretary Freeman presented a bottle of champagne to Soviet Premier Nikita Khrushchev during negotiations for wheat sales to Russia in 1963. Negotiations toward a nuclear-test-ban treaty also were in progress at the time.

11

Toward Global Food Policy

Lyndon Johnson and Orville Freeman learned in the first year of the U.S. pledge to shield the people of India from famine that preempting famine is possible but the protocol for the task requires the commitment of many nations, especially the United States, to wrench policy changes over time. All this became apparent in the second year of the rescue, as President Johnson drove U.S. policy forward. The institutions of American government began scrambling to keep up, unsure of where they were going.

One effect of the new determination to avoid famine was the mobilization of developed and developing nations in support of preemption. Another was that in the following years, preemption emerged as a priority issue in major institutions of global governance. Johnson encouraged that priority if for no other reason than that the process would preoccupy public attention in the United States and the world.

Secretary Freeman's clear-eyed assessment of the status of the United States and India pledges in the Treaty of Rome was a wake-up call. In managing U.S. abundance through the Treaty of Rome, Secretary Freeman had scaled an impressive organizational mountain only to discover that a higher peak lay in wait—the vulnerability of that achievement to fatigue in India. Freeman acknowledged that his earlier optimism was premature, that success was a long-term goal. Without the strength implicit in institutional support a political backlash might threaten the preemption of famine, the central purpose of Johnson's new policy.

Building an institutional framework became a top priority that President Johnson approached as a political task as 1967 began. In late December 1966 he had requested that congressional leaders create a bipartisan panel on the India famine, headed by midwestern agricultural leaders Senator Dole and Representative Poage.

The congressional group quickly found it had ventured into uncertain policy territory and wondered what it was expected to do, what issues it should consider. Poage, who became chair of the House Agriculture Committee in 1967, had the pragmatic answer.

"The real issue is what President Johnson wants to do," he said.

Johnson wanted the congressional panel to evaluate conditions in India independently—for Congress—and to advise him as to whether the United States should agree to pending requests from the government of India for U.S. grain in 1967. The president asked the congressional leaders to participate in a briefing on January 9 with Secretaries Rusk and Freeman and other top administration officials to review the status of the program in India.

The ostensible purpose of the briefing was to discuss interim allocation and timing of U.S. grain shipments so as to ensure a continuing flow of grain under the authority of the earlier congressional resolution endorsing the India program. Johnson said he was planning to make recommendations for the program in his January 23 State of the Union speech to Congress and wanted advice from the assembled group.

Johnson knew that Poage had said the congressional committee would endorse the interim allocations, but the president did not disclose that he had decided to internationalize the U.S. preemption policy. In response to Johnson's initiative, the World Bank had agreed to form a consortium of developed countries to provide half of the assistance needed by India in 1967.

Three days after the January 9 meeting, Johnson held another internal meeting on India with Rusk, Freeman, and other top administration officials to reveal his larger strategy for preemption. After lengthy discussion, the group agreed to a new policy to advance preemption of famine:

1. The World Bank consortium would assume responsibility for half of 1967 food aid to India with the Agency for International Development (AID) to act as the U.S. contact point.

2. The United States would provide 6 million tons of grain, mostly wheat, out of a package of 10 million tons, including cash and fertilizer equivalent.

3. India would be informed of the above decisions, and the United States would determine whether the World Bank consortium could meet 50 percent of a 10 million ton target

4. The president would go to Congress with a January 23 State of the Union message on "Freedom from Hunger" as a U.S. goal.

5. An interim grain allocation with two delivery periods would be adopted with a million tons allocated immediately and a second million tons allocated upon congressional approval

6. Rusk and Freeman would clear the second interim allocation with congressional leaders and the House and Senate appropriations committees.

The State Department was instructed to inform U.S. embassies of the new India initiative by departmental cable. It included a schedule of pledges, ranging from $27 million by Germany and $26 million from Britain to $75,000 from Belgium, that the United States expected other countries to meet. Overall, the United States sought World Bank pledges of more than $150 million.

Eugene Rostow, undersecretary of state for political affairs, would deliver the president's message in person on a schedule of briefings in world capitals to begin immediately, with India. Rostow was to preview in his briefings the message President Johnson intended for his State of the Union address on January 23.

While the world's population had continued to increase, Johnson would say, world food production had fallen sharply behind the rate of population growth.

Vast regions had dropped behind over the past 20 years, Eugene Rostow would explain, even while the United States had brought its domestic surpluses under control. It could no longer be counted on to provide an inexhaustible reservoir of food grain for the hungry as a by-product of domestic policy. The United States expected other nations to shoulder their share of the fight against hunger and malnutrition.

The United States, Rostow explained further, would propose that future food and agricultural aid be coordinated, planned, and allocated insofar as possible through a World Bank consortium. The United States pledged to shoulder half of the aid to the government of India after mid-1967.

In essence, the United States would announce a basic structural goal of global food policy—that is, world food reserves, built from increased domestic production of food in all countries, with the capacity to preempt famine through the ability of commodity trading firms to gather and focus on grain supplies where starvation was threatened.

On January 16 President Johnson sent a letter to Prime Minister Indira Gandhi via the U.S. embassy in New Delhi explaining that he believed India's needs were an international problem and should be met through an international effort. Johnson said he was sending Eugene Rostow as his personal emissary to discuss whether the World Bank consortium was agreeable to India as a concept.

Gandhi brushed off the president. She thanked Johnson in reply but said she would be too busy campaigning for her reelection to see Rostow.[1] She said she wanted the president to know India was committed to increasing food production and controlling population growth. In effect, the prime minister told Johnson that India has its own policies and programs: it was a sovereign nation that could make its own decisions. She was clearly upset that Johnson was telling her what to do rather than proposing that the two nations approach the World Bank together.

Johnson later complained to Freeman that Indira Gandhi was prickly beyond a clash between two strong-willed personalities. The program to preempt the India famine forced a change in relationship: India had come to the United States. Earlier the United States, if it wanted to influence that's country's policy, had to go to India to seek the government's attention.

In most cases, State Department documents show, the United States enticed India—and Pakistan—with a shopping list of military hardware, especially tanks. From India's perspective, the movement of grain from the United States to India was primarily a management arrangement skillfully handled by Freeman. From Johnson's perspective, the government of India should be reminded of the directional flow of the relationship that prevailed between two friendly but powerful nations, an advantage Johnson controlled by insisting that he personally authorized any and all increments of U.S. grain shipments.

The U.S. embassy and the government of India focused on the timing of PL-480 authorizations and the grain shipments, issues that also consumed the time and attention of the U.S. president. During negotiations over congressional support and planning for the 1967

State of the Union address, a delay in authorization threatened the scheduled loading and departure of grain shipments and thus the continuing food deliveries to India. President Johnson personally called the USDA staff members responsible for contracting cargo ships and loading schedules to quietly authorize shipments that would be formally announced later. Whenever Johnson was unable to reach Secretary Freeman to discuss shipping matters, he called the program staff directly for information. Later he chided Freeman, saying that the secretary was never available when the president needed him.

Johnson's tendency toward micromanagement also took him far afield for advice when he was considering the incremental approval of grain shipments. Midway in 1967, as he dithered over a 1.5 million ton authorization of wheat, the president asked George Ball, a former undersecretary of state who by that time was a Wall Street banker at Lehman Brothers, for advice.

"Providing grain is not a humanitarian question but how the government of India uses its finite store of resources," Ball told the president. "India is now using its resources injudiciously, for example, in defense and development. If they had the will to do so, the Indians should be able to find the additional 1.5 million ton of wheat by simply cutting out some of the floss. Based on Middle East and Vietnam policy, they have not earned the right to special consideration on the basis of performance."

Ball said Johnson "should not worry about the reaction of other donors. We have carried this burden, and they have done damn little. Much of the matching they have offered is actually debt relief. In fact, most of India's debt will have to be rolled over indefinitely." And the question of matching was irrelevant, in any event: "The United States is not legally bound to the agreement to match other donor pledges through the World Bank consortium."

Ball concluded, however: "The realistic option is to authorize one-half or two-thirds of the government of India request. This is a generous offer. It should go far to enable India to meet its food requirement and protect foreign exchange resources for development."

Ball had reminded Johnson that he could do whatever he wanted to do but that the National Security Council hotly disputed his specific rationale. "Discounting debt as a match is arbitrary," the council said, "and can't be justified. Further, diminishing debt relief as a form of aid would be viewed by other nations as welching. If the United States insists [that a] 50/50 match is the basis for policy, we will have to break our word if we do otherwise. We need to do more."

The National Security Council said the 50/50 policy was a wrong decision, primarily because it restricted U.S. flexibility. It advised Johnson to treat any U.S. response to the current request as an interim step and proposed he follow Ball's advice to partially approve India's request—two-thirds of the 1.5 million-ton ask as an interim action pending further review. The monsoon season was beginning, and the full scale of need would be apparent in October.

Johnson's special assistant in handling the India/Pakistan policy area—Walt Rostow—reminded the president that further delay on the Indian request would have political consequences.[2] Approval of a million-ton shipment would be enough to avoid serious political unrest and human misery, he said. Further, Rostow acknowledged, "We cannot refuse to help." And he noted that the approval of India's request would protect the president "against charges he is cutting food aid to take the cost of inflation out of the hide of farmers by letting commodity prices fall."

Sensing President Johnson might have second thoughts about the policy of preempting famine, Walt Rostow described what the president had achieved with his new position:

1. Major wheat-producing countries now acknowledge responsibility for food aid. Australia and Canada have shifted perspective—food aid is not dependent on the availability of food surpluses.

2. France, Japan, Germany, Scandinavia, Belgium, the United Kingdom, the Netherlands, and Italy accept the legitimacy of food aid as the responsibility of developed countries.

3. The new policy has enabled India to move from centralized planning, relaxing bureaucratic control of agriculture and farming.

4. Agricultural policy has been imbedded as a priority in India.

5. The World Bank has engaged in food-aid programs for the first time, a priority that will continue because it enlarges the bank's mandate.

6. Major commitments of food aid can continue without raising domestic food price concerns.

The rains came to India in 1967 as the annual monsoons returned in August and September, raising India's wheat production estimates for 1968 to about 95 million tons, with per capita food availability returning nearly to the more adequate levels prevailing in 1964–65. The drought was breaking, and the relationship that had prevailed for three years between the United States and India was changing.

Though grain shipments were no longer needed to forestall famine, India would continue to need more than normal assistance for several reasons, Freeman realized. India's population was increasing, and the country would probably have 50 million more stomachs to fill in 1968 than in 1964. And India's normal reserves—the grain required to assure relatively stable food markets—had been deployed to contain the famine. India's food cupboard was nearly empty. The USDA's projections of India's agricultural output, even with the changes adopted under the Treaty of Rome agreement, did not show a stable balance of India's store of grain with domestic consumption until 1970.

Secretary Freeman also wanted to ensure the continuation of the Treaty of Rome reforms. The reports of localized food shortages and hunger occurring in 1967 raised some concern on this issue. Over-all grain supplies were adequate in 1967 to maintain minimum per capita food availability, but in some areas state government hoarding had blocked access to supplies. Under Indian law, state governments could block shipments of food, grain, and farm production materials out of state territory. The policy of unimpeded interstate commerce did not exist in India in the 1960s. State government could impose zonal border policies to restrict the movement of food, a practice defeating the best efforts of the United States and the government of India to guard against famine. Freeman wanted India to abolish such zones.

In October President Johnson and Secretary Freeman met with Ambassador Nehru to discuss prospective commitments for grain shipments in 1968 and the status of the Treaty of Rome agreement as a preliminary to future action through the World Bank consortium. Noting the population growth of India and the need to rebuild grain reserves, Freeman said the United States was willing to ship 3.5 million tons of grain through the first half of 1968 as a PL-480 concessional sale to ensure continued grain availability. The United States, Freeman said, estimated India would need grain imports of about 9.5 million tons, including 2 million tons in private stocks to rebuild reserves another 2 million in government-held reserves.

The system of zonal boundaries employed by state governments in India, Freeman said, restricted the movement of food in India. People living in food-surplus areas were needlessly exposing Indians in deficit states to hunger and starvation. In addition, zonal restrictions were impeding the development of food reserves, and Freeman said he wanted India to abolish zonal restrictions.

Ambassador Nehru agreed that Freeman's estimates of grain-import needs in 1968 were in line with the government of India's calculations. He said India was projecting that wheat production in 1968 would exceed 95 million tons, the highest level since 1964. Nehru demurred from the proposal to abolish zonal restrictions on the movement of food, arguing that the action would be politically unwise given the still fresh memory of impending famine. He said he would report the views of the U.S. government to the prime minister and respond soon to the president and the secretary.

A month later Nehru said the government of India was in basic agreement with the United States on its proposal for 1968 and the food situation going forward—aside from abolishing the food zones. The ambassador did pledge that India would end the food zones at the end of 1968.

Left unsaid in this exchange was what conditions would apply to the 3.5 million tons of India's wheat imports during the last half of 1968. As the National Security Council had concluded earlier, the 50/50 arrangement for future food aid under the World Bank consortium limited future U.S. options regarding the conditions of commercial trade. Other developed countries had joined the bank consortium only under condition the United States forgo the opportunity to link gifts, or conditional sales, to commercial grain sales. The United States could not say that the PL-480 sale of wheat—a gift to India—required India to agree to buy another 3.5 million tons of wheat for cash.

In late 1967, relations between India and the United States were returning to normal, but they would never be the same as in the years preceding 1965. India needed food assistance, but it was rapidly expanding food production as a result of the Treaty of Rome. And it was quickly building foreign exchange resources as the grip of famine fell away, allowing the county to explore with other nations its willingness to pay cash for grain imports. Reports of these conversations had already reached the grain trade.

In the United States, wheat farmers were anticipating a wheat crop in 1968 of more than a billion bushels of wheat, a crop Secretary Freeman knew would sell for less than $1.40 to $1.50 a bushel unless the

United States could sell 500 million bushels in concessional sales or commercial exports.

With the potential India famine abated, American wheat farmers were expecting the secretary of agriculture to worry less about world hunger and more about grain sales management.

The Freemans "up north" after Orville's retirement from government service. After leaving the Johnson administration, he was chief executive of two information companies—EDP Technology, then Business International Corporation. From 1985 to 1995, he headed up the Washington, D.C., office of a Minneapolis law firm. Upon returning to Minneapolis in 1995, he became a visiting scholar at the Hubert H. Humphrey Institute of Public Affairs. He died at age 84 in 2003.

12

Conclusion

Orville L. Freeman was one of the longest-serving (1961–1969) secretaries of agriculture in U.S. history. He worked with two strong-willed presidents with sharply differing styles, both relying on him for advice and supporting his advocacy for major policy changes. His strong leadership style, close relationships with Congress, command of detail, and drive for change in the public interest were characteristic of his eight years as secretary. His strong commitment to boosting farm income and enhancing rural economic development coupled with his focused effort to help reduce world hunger and use food to enhance world peace. *World without Hunger* was not only a driving force but also the title of one of the several books he wrote.

Freeman hit the road running in 1961, helping President Kennedy fulfill a campaign promise by reconstituting the Food Stamp program with ten demonstration projects funded not with new tax dollars but with existing revenues found in a tariff account in the USDA budget. His revised program reduced the waste and bureaucracy that had plagued earlier food distribution systems. Today, the Food Stamp program (now SNAP) feeds more than 45 million Americans every day. In addition, Freeman led reforms that brought school lunch and breakfast programs and the Women, Infants and Children (WIC) system to millions more hungry people. These major programs to alleviate domestic hunger in the 1960s are still critical today.

Freeman faced the paradox of huge food surpluses and low farm prices at home while huge population increases and food shortages loomed overseas. As one of the two architects of the Treaty of Rome, he demonstrated how cooperative public policy can alleviate the disastrous effects of drought and preempt widespread famine. This effort influenced future policies of the World Bank and United Nations agencies as well as those of the United States and India to enhance food production and reduce global hunger.

At home, Freeman insisted upon high standards in the enforcement of consumer food protection laws, and he helped stop a potential massive intrusion into primitive forestlands. He substantially improved the management of public uses of national parks and forests through cooperation with Secretary of the Interior Stuart Udall.

Orville Freeman was a passionate friend of the American farmer and rural citizens. He was a dedicated environmentalist and watchdog of the food we eat. But most of all, he was an internationalist dedicated to developing agriculture worldwide and to helping feed the world's hungry. A Marine and a liberal, Freeman led with ideas and passion. His was a career and a life of committed public service.

Epilogue

In 2014, American farmers harvested record crops of corn, soybeans and wheat, but some see this achievement as more a going back to the future than a national accomplishment. The United States has been there and done that, most recently in 1961. Grain production then, particularly corn at some 9 billion bushels, had never been greater, and it confronted Americans with a conundrum of rising material abundance in the face, for many, of a loss of personal financial wealth.

With the books closed on crop production in 2014, corn output exceeded 14.4 billion bushels and soybean production topped 3.9 billion bushels. Demand for both corn and soybeans is expected to be strong in 2015—for consumption as food, for use as feed to produce milk, meat and poultry, for conversion to ethanol, and for export to global markets. Some 1.6 billion bushels, however, are left as surplus to be added to U.S. stock, now with carryover levels in excess of 2 billion bushels. The data for soybeans are similar, with U.S. carryover the largest in 10 years.

Some people will find the figures dazzling, but one consequence of such surplus means a decrease of farm net income of nearly $30 billion. Corn and soybean prices at local grain elevators across the Mississippi River watershed ranged from $3 to $4 a bushel lower in October 2014 than earlier that year.

Fifty years ago, around the time when Orville Freeman became secretary of agriculture, farm surpluses were a highly charged political issue for the American people. Shock was visible in news reports showing giant corn piles lying open in the streets of midwestern towns and giving rise to discussion of mountains of grain, lakes of milk, and castles of butter. The grain providing the visual symbols of surplus disappeared into storage and declined under the effect of new farm legislation, proposed by President Kennedy and Secretary Freeman. After a century of policy promoting agricultural abundance, the government made a profound shift to managing abundance through supply management, an innovation promoted by Freeman.

This policy of supply management, sometimes controversial and often criticized, has been the guiding concept for the U.S. agricultural economy, particularly as to corn, wheat, and beans, over the past half-century. Managed abundance might be described, as Churchill once said about democracy, as the worst system of governance in farm policy—except all others.

This changed early in 2014. Congress replaced supply management with crop insurance, a program to encourage farmers and farm corporations to purchase an insurance contract from a private insurance company that guarantees a negotiated price for a particular crop at harvest.

Under the new policy, the federal government eliminated several programs, including that of paying cash to farmers contracting with the USDA not to produce certain crops or claiming loss of income from specific growing conditions. The federal government does not pay farmers or farm corporations to offset the cost of insurance contracts but does pay large subsidies to insurance companies, in effect lowering the cost of the contracts.

This shift from the Freeman-led policy of supply management begun in the 1960s to the new insurance model is fundamental and profound. Many question this radical shift. Whether it can meet the surplus crisis of 2014 and 2015 and respond to future market developments better than the supply management model remains to be seen.

The experiment with crop insurance also exposes a dual fault line in American governance that began growing in the last half of the 20th century, one related to the function of cabinet officers and the other to the organization of congressional committees.

Secretary Freeman led the development of major policy changes in agriculture, identifying the potential for the creative expansion of departmental authority to better serve the needs of an increasingly urban economy and to eliminate poverty as a cause of hunger and chronic malnutrition. He also used food as a weapon of world peace. Expanding rural economic development was also a cornerstone of his eight years as the secretary of agriculture.

Freeman modernized the managerial system of a huge government agency. He was both an innovator and a manager, while today's cabinet officers are expected to act primarily as managers. The executive authority of the federal government has collapsed inward to the Office of the President. This has accompanied the stunning inability of Congress to innovate during a period of astonishing change in the U.S. and global economies. The agriculture committees continue to legislate as if their constituencies were farmers, farm families, and the farm economy, even though farmers are a minority group even in rural areas and farm employment continues to shrink.

The world needs access to the abundance of American agriculture, and U.S. farmers and communities need financial stability. The adoption of crop insurance as the primary economic policy in agriculture illustrates the inability of Congress to address dysfunctional conflict. One can but wonder what tools Freeman might have used to face the current surplus.

Appendix A

A Short History
of Federal Food Initiatives

The First Food Stamp Program, May 16, 1939–Spring 1943

The idea of the first food stamp program (FSP) is credited to various people, most notably Secretary of Agriculture Henry Wallace and the program's first administrator, Milo Perkins. The program operated by permitting people on relief to buy orange stamps equal to their normal food expenditures. For each dollar's worth of orange stamps purchased, 50 cents' worth of blue stamps was received. Orange stamps could buy any food. Blue stamps could buy food determined by the department to be surplus.

Over the course of nearly four years, the first food stamp program reached approximately 20 million people in nearly half of the counties in the United States at one time or another. Peak participation was 4 million—at a total cost of $262 million. The first recipient was Mabel McFiggin of Rochester, New York. The first retailer to redeem the stamps was Joseph Mutolo. The first retailer caught violating the program was Nick Salzano, in October 1939. The program ended when the conditions bringing the program into existence—widespread unemployment and unmarketable food surpluses—no longer existed.

Pilot Food Stamp Program—May 29, 1961–1964

The 18 years between the end of the first FSP and the inception of the next were filled with studies, reports, and legislative proposals. Prominent senators actively associated with attempts to enact an FSP during this period were: George Aiken (R-V), Robert M. La Follette Jr. (R-W), Hubert Humphrey (D-MN), Estes Kefauver (D-TN), and Stuart Symington (D-MO). From 1954 forward, Congresswoman Leonor K. Sullivan (D-MO) strove unceasingly to pass food stamp program legislation. On September 21, 1959, Public Law (PL) 86-341 authorized the secretary of agriculture to operate a food stamp system through January 31, 1962.

The Eisenhower administration never used the authority. But in fulfillment of a campaign promise made in West Virginia, President Kennedy's first executive order called for expanded food distribution. On February 2, 1961, he announced that food stamp pilot programs would be initiated. The pilot programs would retain the requirement that the food stamps be purchased, but they eliminated the concept of special stamps for surplus foods. A department spokesman indicated the emphasis would be on increasing the consumption of perishables. Isabelle Kelley, who was part of the four-person team that designed the new program, became its first director and the first woman in USDA to head an action program.

Alderson and Chloe Muncy of Paynesville, West Virginia, were the first food stamp recipients, on May 29, 1961. They purchased $95 in food stamps for their 15-person household. In the first food stamp transaction, they bought a can of pork and beans at Henderson's Supermarket. By January 1964, the pilot programs had expanded from 8 areas to 43 (40 counties plus Detroit, St. Louis, and Pittsburgh) in 22 states with 380,000 participants.

Food Stamp Act of 1964—August 31, 1964

On January 31, 1964, President Lyndon B. Johnson requested that Congress pass legislation making the food stamp program permanent. Secretary of Agriculture Freeman submitted legislation for that purpose on April 17, 1964. The bill eventually passed was H.R. 10222, introduced by Rep. Leonor Sullivan. Among the official purposes of the Food Stamp Act of 1964 were strengthening the agricultural economy and improving levels of nutrition among low-income households. Its practical purpose was to bring the pilot FSP under congressional control and to enact the regulations into law. Its major provisions were:

- the State Plan of Operation requirement and the development of eligibility standards by the states
- the purchase of food stamps by recipients paying an amount commensurate with their normal expenditures for food, which ostensibly would provide them a low-cost, nutritionally adequate diet
- the eligibility for purchase with food stamps of all items intended for human consumption except alcoholic beverages and imported foods (The House version would have prohibited soft drinks, luxury foods, and luxury frozen foods.)
- the prohibition of discrimination on the basis of race, religious creed, national origin, or political beliefs
- the division of responsibilities between the state (certification and issuance) and federal (funding of benefits and authorization of retailers and wholesalers) governments, with shared responsibility for funding the costs of administration
- appropriations for the first year limited to $75 million, for the second year to $100 million, and the third to $200 million

The department estimated that the national food stamp program would eventually reach 4 million people, at an annual cost of $360 million.

Appendix B

The Treaty of Rome

Rome, December 26, 1965*
Title: Agreement between Secretary of Agriculture Orville L. Freeman
and Minister of Food and Agriculture C. Subramaniam, November
1965, Rome, Italy

It was agreed that it was very much to the benefit of both India
and the United States to reverse the disturbing downward trend in the
per capita food production.

It was agreed that the quantity of resources allocated to agriculture
has not been adequate in recent years.

---

*From Office of the Historian, U.S. Department of State, *Foreign Relations
of the United States of America, 1961–1968*, Vol. 25, *South Asia*. Washington,
D.C.: U.S. Government Printing Office. Available online, regularly updated.

It was agreed that:

1. Investment in agriculture during the fourth Five Year Plan, 1966–67 to 1970–71, will be 2,400 crore rupees or more than double the investment levels during the third plan period ending this year.
2. Investment in agriculture during the coming year [1966–67] will be increased by at least 40 percent above the current year even though the emergency might require cutbacks in other areas of investment.
3. Investment in agriculture next year [1967–68] will be 410 crore rupees as against 304 crore rupees this year.

It was agreed that:

1. The Government of India will publicly announce and endorse the fertilizer consumption targets for the next 5 years agreed to by the Indian Minister of Food and Agriculture. These quantities of fertilizer, to be made available through imports, if domestic production is inadequate, are as follows:

YEAR	N	P205 (MILLION METRIC TON)	K20
1966–67	1.00	0.37	0.20
1967–68	1.35	0.50	0.30
1968–69	1.708	0.65	0.45
1969–70	2.00	0.80	0.55
1970–71	2.40	1.00	0.70

2. Basic policy changes encouraging foreign private investment in the manufacture and distribution of fertilizer will be implemented.

   a. The Government of India will announce a plan before January 1, 1966, to purchase any fertilizer produced in excess of market demand at world market prices.

   b. The Government of India will announce the removal of any geographic constrains on fertilizer marketing before January 1, 1966, to take effect as soon as fertilizer supplies are adequate, now expected in 1968-69.

   c. The Government of India will reduce the role of the central nitrogen pool from its present near-monopoly position to one in which it handles only a minor part of the fertilizer supply. All manufacturers of nitrogenous fertilizer will be authorized to establish their own distribution arrangements.

3. That steps will be taken by the government to operate its own fertilizer plants at full capacity by allocation of enough foreign exchange to ensure adequate supplies of raw materials and spare parts and by carefully reviewing periodically the level of management effectiveness.

4. That if modifications in the procedures for approving and licensing foreign private investment in the manufacture and distribution of fertilizer do not sufficiently shorten the time required for negotiations, further administrative and procedural changes will be made.

5. A cabinet-level committee, now chaired by the Prime Minister, will make a continuing effort to see that bureaucratic procedures do not hinder or discourage private foreign investment in fertilizer production and distribution. It will also pass judgment on basic policy questions which if unresolved might hinder investment.

6. That there will be no tie-in between credit and distribution. That is, farmers will be given credit regardless of where they buy their fertilizer.

7. That the Government of India will not require government participation in the ownership of fertilizer plants in the private sector.

It was agreed that the current system of credit cooperatives is not adequate and the following actions will be taken to remedy this:

1. A cabinet-level committee on agricultural credit chaired by the Food and Agricultural Minister will explore alternative avenues of supplying credit to farmers.
2. The government will systematically review and test alternative credit possibilities. The following will be tested on a pilot basis:
   a. The food corporation will supply credit to farmers against advances on their crops.
   b. Current private credit institutions will be urged to extend credit availability and the possible need for credit subsidies will be evaluated.
3. The possibility of an all-India agricultural credit organization to supplement the credit supply of the cooperative sector will be actively explored.

It was agreed that the new instrumentalities, such as the agricultural production board, a committee of cabinet members, and other key officials chaired by the Food and Agricultural Minister and vested with the authority to make binding decisions on matters of agricultural production, will be used to achieve the necessary allocation of resources in Indian agriculture.

It was agreed that:

1. 32 million acres of the most productive land farmed by the more efficient farmers will be designated for a crash production program with a target of 25 million tons of additional food grains by 1970 on this selected acreage.

2. The resources and inputs necessary will have the number-one priority to wit:

    a. The new fertilizer responsive varieties of food grain will be planted on well-irrigated land, applying from 100 to 150 pounds of fertilizer per acre as compared with a national average of 3 to 5 pounds per acre. These new varieties, planted on the best irrigated land, will get the necessary fertilizer even though this might require a cutback of some other land if fertilizer were in short supply.

    b. If the seed multiplication programs for the new imported varieties (wheat from Mexico and rice from the International Rice Research Institute in the Philippines) fall behind schedule, foreign exchange will be made available for the import of additional suitable seed.

    c. New irrigation techniques, going from the traditional flow method to controlled maximum irrigation, will be selectively applied. For this purpose resources will be made available whenever it is demonstrated practicable. In addition, adequate resources will be made available to develop irrigation sources to attain a water balance multiple cropping. With this new intensive irrigation more and more land will be double cropped.

It was agreed that the price policies will be reviewed periodically to ensure a continuing favorable relationship between the price of food grains and the price of purchased inputs such as fertilizer.

It was concluded that the new legislation establishing the food corporation and the recent amendments to the Defense of India rules along with the basic constitutional provisions did give the central government adequate authority to control the movement and distribution of grain between the states. The Minister made it clear that the central government has the authority to develop and implement a national food policy.

It was agreed that efforts to dramatize and mobilize public sentiment to demonstrate the urgency of action in agriculture will be made. Such action as public statements by the President, Prime Minister and other leading public officials will be used even more in the future.

It was agreed that:

1. Highest priority will be given to agricultural development and allied programs in the fourth Five Year Plan. This priority also will apply to the allocation of foreign exchange to agriculture. It is noted that the agriculture program detailed above will require foreign exchange of the order of 2 billion dollars for the fourth Five Year Plan.
2. To meet food production targets the import of 500,000 tons of nitrogen fertilizer for the 1966–67 crop is essential. Out of the total quantity needed, arrangements will be made to import 100,000 tons from available resources. Every effort will be made to find the balance of the resources required to reach the target. Minister Subramaniam emphasized the critical importance of reaching the target, starting that in view of severe limits on the availability of foreign exchange that immediate United States aid is imperative.

It was agreed that the Government of India will make the following food aid phase-out schedule an integral part of the fourth Five Year Plan for agriculture:

Year	Cereal Deficit	Import Requirements For Buffer Stock (In million tons)	Import Requirements
1965–66	Minus 6.2	0.8	7.0
1966–67	Minus 3.8	1.2	5.5
1967–68	Minus 2.0	2.0	4.0
1968–69	Minus 0.2	2.3	2.5
1969–70	Minus 0.9	nil	nil

Signed:

Orville L. Freeman, Secretary of Agriculture, United States of America

C. Subramaniam, Minster of Food and Agriculture, India

Dated November 25, 1965

Notes

Chapter 1: Awakening

1. Kennedy had called Freeman the morning after the election, saying he hoped Freeman would join the New Frontier, without specifying the capacity. Freeman called him "Mr. President" from the day he was elected.

Chapter 2: Taking Over

1. Sen. Hubert H. Humphrey, whose bid for the presidential nomination had flamed out in West Virginia and Wisconsin, was the nominal Minnesota delegation leader, but he would not lead the delegation to support any potential candidate other than himself, leaving the delegation to splinter indecisively until Kennedy won the nomination on the first ballot.
2. Johnson, after his election to the presidency in 1964, acknowledged that Kennedy's alternate choice of running mate was Freeman. The two men were relaxing by the swimming pool at the presidential retreat Camp David, in September 1965, when Johnson suddenly spoke: "You know, you should been here instead of me. Do you know how I know? Kennedy

told me. He said he had chosen to name you as his vice president if I declined his offer." Neither Freeman nor Johnson mentioned this to the other again.

3. William Jardine and Henry Wallace, earlier secretaries of agriculture. Author's recollection of a personal conversation in Whitten's House office with David Frederickson, then president of the National Farmers Union. Frederickson is at the time of this writing Minnesota's commissioner of agriculture.

Chapter 3: Inventing American Food Policy

1. WIC is the acronym for the Women, Infant, and Children program that provides monthly food supplements and nutrition counseling for pregnant women and for mothers and their children under age 5, the period of life when physical and intellectual growth is most vulnerable to malnutrition. In the decade from 1990 to 2000, the WIC program served nearly half of all infants born in the United States at some time during their first five years. WIC currently assists nearly 9 million individuals, including more than 4 million infants and children under age 5, at an annual cost of almost $10 billion.

2. Although widespread fraud was contained through vigorous enforcement, merchants and participants tested the USDA's resolve to minimize abuse. An under-the-counter market for food stamps developed early, with buyers and sellers discounting stamps at 50 cents on the dollar. Some grocery retailers boldly made bank deposits of bundles of certificates worth more than the grocery sales for the sale period claimed.

3. The 30 percent was an estimate by Molly Orshansky, an economist in the Bureau of Labor Statistics, of the proportion of spending for food by families and individuals at poverty levels. The proportion was later calculated more precisely, using more relevant statistical models.

4. As the year 2011 began, more than 45 million people in America participated in the food stamp program, now entitled by Congress as SNAP (Supplemental Nutritional Assistance Program). This bureaucratically pleasing title committed the United States only to an effort to eliminate hunger. Statisticians estimated another 15 to 20 percent of the U.S. population was eligible but did not apply for help.

5. The department was renamed Health and Human Services (HHS) upon creation of the Department of Education as a cabinet-level entity.

Chapter 4: Supply Management

1. Cochrane was a leading agricultural economist at the University of Minnesota in 1960. As an adviser to Governor Freeman, he chaired a governor's commission in 1958 that produced a seminal study on agricultural policy focusing on supply management. He was a leading scholar on agricultural policy and traveled as an adviser on agriculture to John F. Kennedy when he was campaigning for president in 1960. Cochrane's interests included food policy, especially the food stamp program operated in the Agriculture Department briefly before World War II. He served as chief agricultural economist in the USDA for three years before returning to his farm economist post at the university.

2. Here and below, *New York Times,* January 4, 1961, p. 1.

3. The Administrative Procedures Act, proposed by President Harry S. Truman and adopted by Congress in 1948, was innovative in federal policy management. Managing the complex array of services Congress authorized during the Roosevelt presidency required administrative authority from Congress that often languished in congressional committees in dispute, often petty argument, and procedural conflict. The inability of Congress to settle them promptly caused delays in service to the public and added public costs that could have been avoided.

   Leaders of Congress agreed with President Truman that administrative issues could be better resolved through procedures that allowed for a timely review of executive proposals by Congress, after which administrative measures would be automatically adopted if Congress did not object. A process that now requires public review and comment on regulatory rules and procedures before adoption evolved from this concept. Congress adopted a somewhat similar procedure in 1936, authorizing dairy farmers and producers of specialty crops to develop orderly market conditions, establish product standards, and agree to adopt minimum product prices. Market orders adopted by two-thirds of producers in specified geographical areas and managed by the USDA have been established generally to cover fluid milk and a limited number of specialty crops.

4. Freeman papers, 1964, the John F. Kennedy Presidential Library, Boston.

5. Freeman personal diary, Minnesota Historical Society.

6. Secretary Freeman memo to the files, Kennedy papers, John F. Kennedy Presidential Library, Boston.

7. Freeman was especially mindful of his good friend and political ally Senator Humphrey, who was urging the White House to roll out a new wheat program proposal almost as soon as the outcome of the 1963 referendum

became clear. Political allies agree on goals but often argue over timing.

Chapter 5: President Kennedy Is Dead: A First-Hand Account

1. Freeman's jaw was severely damaged by a Japanese sniper's bullet while he was leading a Marine patrol on Bougainville Island in November 1943.
2. Shortly before announcing that he chose Lyndon Johnson as his running mate for the 1960 campaign, Kennedy asked Freeman and his wife, Jane, to come to his Los Angeles hotel suite. He told them he had considered nominating Freeman for the vice presidency should Johnson decline the honor and that he hoped Freeman would support Johnson's candidacy.
3. Jane Freeman recalls making hot chocolate for Sorensen and Governor Freeman.
4. In September 1963, the Republican-led Senate Rules Committee had opened an investigation of Baker's business and political activities (for allegations including bribery and trading sexual favors for votes and government contracts). He resigned as secretary of the Senate in October.

Chapter 7: Defending the Land and Its People

1. Secretary of Agriculture Earl Butz forcefully articulated the latter approach later, during the Nixon administration. "Get big or get out," he warned farmers.
2. OEO financed nonprofit advocacy groups and city projects that criticized USDA-funded food programs, urging states to do more and the USDA to expand services faster. State governments and the USDA agreed with these suggestions, wryly noting that OEO was using federal funds that could be spent to serve more people and expand food programs faster.

Chapter 9: Confronting Famine and Saving Democracy

1. *See* Appendix B.
2. *See* Appendix B.

Chapter 10: The Political Challenge of Preempting Famine

1. Since 1925 the Office of Historian of the Department of State has published the series *Foreign Relations of the United States,* documenting major foreign policy decisions and significant diplomatic activity of the U.S. government. The series documents facts and events contributing to the formulation of policies and includes evidence of supporting and alternative views to the policy positions adopted. Volume 25, *South Asia,* covers

U.S. foreign policy activities in South Asia over the 1964–1968 period, when the Johnson administration adopted a preemptive strategy to block famine on the India subcontinent, leading to major foreign policy changes. Orville L. Freeman's role in these activities is described in detail.

2. The USDA had two banking agencies: Agricultural Stabilization and Conservation Service (ASCS, merged in 1994 with other USDA services into the Farm Service Agency) made loans to farmers for which the collateral was the crop of the borrowing farmer upon harvest. The grain was stored, and ASCS took title to the commodity when the contract was closed. If the market price at closure was less than that when the loan was made, ASCS became the owner of the commodity, absorbing the loss. If the market price was higher, the farmer could pay off the loan and pocket the difference.

   The other USDA bank was Farmers Home Administration (FmHA), making low-interest loans to farmers and holding their farmland as collateral. The loans were mostly for production costs, and production loans were the most common form of farming credit. Under the loan agreement, a farmer was eligible for future loans if he or she paid off the present one. If he did not, FmHA could take ownership of the land through foreclosure and sell the land. The farmer absorbed the loss, losing the farm.

   In either case, the USDA bank lost funds and had to ask Congress to replenish its budget. Bankers claimed that failure to foreclose on farm loans would cause the banking system to collapse. Over time, ASCS crop loans raised income for farmers, and FHA production loans increased farm consolidation and reduced the number of farmers.

3. Freeman was cautioned by staff aides to avoid any mention of cattle in India when discussing the India famine with Senator Ellender, chairman of the Senate Agriculture Committee, who would erupt in a lecture on "sacred cows" when people in India were starving. Cattle were sacred symbols in India, allowed to wander freely, munching on gardens and food in markets without interference.

Chapter 11: Toward Global Food Policy

1. India held its national elections in February 1967. Minister of Food and Agriculture Subramaniam lost his seat in the India Parliament as did several members of the Congress Party, which returned to Parliament with a diminished majority. Observers argued that the massive food aid from the United States was the dominant factor in preserving the fortunes of the

party. Gandhi's grip on India politics was strengthened, and she served several terms as prime minister until her assassination in 1984 by Sikh groups angered by India's use of military force against them.

2. Walt Rostow had been seconded to the White House from the State Department, where he headed the Office of Planning. He was the brother of Eugene Rostow, undersecretary of state for political affairs.

Index

As Orville Freeman's name appears on virtually every page, only his illustrations, appointments, and positions are indexed by name.

For most names, only the highest elected position or title is noted.

Illustration page numbers are listed first, in italics.

Orville Freeman and author Rod Leonard

About the Author

Rodney E. Leonard served as press secretary to Orville L. Freeman, during the years Freeman was governor of Minnesota (1955–1960) and U.S. secretary of agriculture (1961–1969). Immediately afterward, Leonard founded the Community Nutrition Institute, remaining its head and chief writer on food policy for more than 40 years. Leonard also served in the Carter administration as deputy director of the U.S. Office of Consumer Affairs in 1978–79. He and his wife, Elizabeth Berg Leonard, retired to Betty's family farm near Wahkon, Minnesota, in 1998. Betty died in 2001.